Introduction to
the Letter to the Hebrews

I0149031

Introduction to the Letter to the Hebrews

under the supervision of
David Young

Theological Essentials

Library of Congress Cataloging-in-Publication Data

David Young (creator).
Introduction to the Letter to the Hebrews / David Young
107 + x pp. cm. 12.7 x 20.32
ISBN 979-8-89731-391-4 (Print)
ISBN 979-8-89731-127-9 (Ebook)
ISBN 979-8-89731-128-6 (Kindle)
ISBN 979-8-89731-127-9 (Abridged Audio Discussion)

      1. Bible. N.T. Hebrews — Introductions.
      2. Bible. N.T. Hebrews — Criticism, interpretation, etc.
BS2775.3 .Y68 2025

This book is available in other languages at
www.DTLPress.com

Cover Image: Leaf from an illuminated manuscript of the Epistle to the Hebrews, produced in 1101 by Joannes Koulix
Photo credit: MetMuseum.org image 1991.232.15

DTL

Contents

Series Preface

Artificial Intelligence (AI) is changing everything, including theological scholarship and education. This series, *Theological Essentials*, is designed to bring the creative potential of AI to the field of theological education. In the traditional model, a scholar with both mastery of the scholarly discourse and a record of successful classroom teaching would spend several months—or even several years—writing, revising and rewriting an introductory text which would then be transferred to a publisher who also invested months or years in production processes. Even though the end product was typically quite predictable, this slow and expensive process caused the prices of textbooks to balloon. As a result, students in developed nations paid more than they should have for the books and students in developing nations typically had no access to these (cost-prohibitive) textbooks until they appeared as discards and donations decades later. In previous generations, the need for quality assurance—in the form of content generation, expert review, copy-editing and printing time—may have made this slow, expensive and exclusionary approach inevitable. However, AI is changing everything.

This series is very different; it is created by AI. The cover of each volume identifies the work as "created under the supervision of" an expert in the field. However, that person is not an author in the traditional sense. The creator of each volume has been trained by the DTL staff in the use of AI and *the creator has used AI to create, edit, revise and recreate the text that you see*. With that creation process clearly identified, let me explain the goals of this series.

Our Goals:

Credibility: Although AI has made — and continues to make — huge strides over the last few years, no unsupervised AI can create a truly reliable or fully credible college or seminary level text. The limitations of AI generated content sometimes originates from the limitations of the content itself (the training set may be inadequate), but more often, user dissatisfaction with AI-generated content arises from human errors associated with poor prompt engineering. The DTL Press has sought to overcome both of these problems by hiring established scholars with widely recognized expertise to create books within their areas of expertise and by training those scholars and experts in AI prompt engineering. To be clear, the scholar whose name appears on the cover of this work has created this volume — generating, reading, regenerating, rereading and revising the work. Even though the work was generated (in varying degrees) by AI, the names of our scholarly creators appear on the cover as a guarantee that the content is equally credible with any introductory work which that scholar/creator would pen using the traditional model.

Affordability: The DTL Press is committed to the idea that affordability should not be a barrier to knowledge. *All persons are equally deserving of the right to know and to understand.* Therefore, ebook versions of all DTL Press books are available from the DTL libraries without charge, and available as print books for a nominal fee. Our scholar/creators are to be thanked for their willingness to forego traditional royalty arrangements. (Our creators are compensated for their generative work, but they do not receive royalties in the traditional sense.)

Accessibility: The DTL Press would like to make high quality, low cost introductory textbooks available to everyone, everywhere in the world. The books in this series are immediately made available in multiple languages. The DTL Press will create translations in other languages upon request. Translations are, of course, generated by AI.

Our Acknowledged Limitations:

Some readers are undoubtedly thinking, "but AI can only produce derivative scholarship; AI can't create original, innovative scholarship." That criticism is, of course, largely accurate. AI is largely limited to aggregating, organizing and repackaging pre-existing ideas (although sometimes in ways that can be used to accelerate and refine the production of original scholarship). Still while acknowledging this inherent limitation of AI, the DTL Press would offer two comments: (1) Introductory texts are seldom meant to be truly ground breaking in their originality and (2) the DTL Press has other series dedicated to publishing original scholarship with traditional authorship.

Our Invitation:

The DTL Press would like to fundamentally reshape academic publishing in the theological world to make scholarship more accessible and more affordable in two ways. First, we would like to generate introductory texts in all areas of theological discourse, so that no one is ever forced to "buy a textbook" in any language. It is our vision for professors anywhere to be able to use one book, two books or an entire set of books in this series as the *introductory* textbooks for their classes. Second, we would also like to publish traditionally authored scholarly monographs for Open Access (free) distribution for an advanced scholarly readership.

Finally, the DTL Press is non-confessional and will publish works in any area of religious studies. Traditionally authored books are peer-reviewed; AI-generated introductory book creation is open to anyone with the required expertise to supervise content generation in that area of discourse. If you share the DTL Press's commitment to credibility, affordability and accessibility, contact us about changing the world of theological publishing by contributing to this series or a more traditionally authored series.

With high expectations,

Thomas E. Phillips

DTL Press Executive Director

www.thedtl.org

Chapter 1
Why Hebrews Matters

The Epistle to the Hebrews occupies a unique and often underappreciated place in the New Testament canon. Neither a traditional epistle nor a gospel narrative, Hebrews defies easy categorization. It reads more like an extended sermon — one that blends rich theological reflection with urgent pastoral exhortation. Its author, whose identity remains unknown, crafts a message of remarkable rhetorical power and scriptural depth. Hebrews speaks simultaneously to the mind and the heart, calling readers to contemplate the majesty of Christ while warning against the spiritual complacency that can lead to apostasy.

At the heart of the epistle lies a majestic portrait of Jesus Christ — Son of God, great High Priest, and mediator of a better covenant. This portrait is constructed through a series of scriptural expositions and comparisons. The author draws extensively on the Old Testament, particularly the Septuagint, to show how Jesus fulfills and surpasses the institutions and figures of Israel's history. From angels and Moses to the Levitical priesthood and the tabernacle, all previous revelations and mediators point forward to Christ.

Several themes emerge prominently throughout the letter:

The Superiority of Christ: Hebrews opens with a powerful affirmation of Christ's divine identity and redemptive mission (Heb. 1:1–4). Jesus is portrayed as the final and definitive revelation of God, superior to angels, prophets, and previous messengers.

The Heavenly Priesthood: Central to the epistle is the depiction of Jesus as a great High Priest, not in the order of Aaron but of Melchizedek. Unlike the earthly priests, who offer repeated sacrifices, Jesus enters the heavenly sanctuary to offer himself once for all (Heb. 4:14–5:10; 7:1–28).

The Fulfillment of Scripture: The author of Hebrews reads the Old Testament Christologically, using figures such as Melchizedek and texts such as Psalm 110 and Jeremiah 31 to argue that Jesus brings to completion God's covenantal purposes.

Perseverance in Faith: Interwoven with theology is a series of urgent pastoral warnings. Believers are exhorted to press on, to hold fast, and to avoid the peril of turning away. These warning passages (e.g., Heb. 2:1–4; 6:4–12; 10:26–31) underscore the seriousness of apostasy and the necessity of endurance.

In addition to its thematic richness, Hebrews is notable for its literary artistry and rhetorical sophistication. The author makes frequent use of rhetorical devices such as inclusio, analogy, and diatribe. The letter is structured in such a way that exposition and exhortation alternate, creating a rhythm that both teaches and persuades. Far from being a dry theological treatise, Hebrews is a dynamic appeal that moves the reader from understanding to response.

Why study Hebrews today? The reasons are manifold:

Theological Depth: Hebrews offers one of the most profound meditations on the person and work of Christ in the New Testament. Its exploration of incarnation, priesthood, atonement, and eschatology invites readers into the mystery and majesty of God's redemptive plan.

Scriptural Interpretation: Few texts in the New Testament demonstrate such a sustained and creative engagement with the Old Testament. Hebrews models a way of reading Scripture that is deeply Christ-centered and theologically robust.

Pastoral Urgency: The epistle was written to people under pressure — tempted to give up or turn back. Its exhortations to hold fast and persevere are as relevant now as they were then, especially in a world where faith is often challenged by suffering, doubt, or cultural marginalization.

Contemporary Relevance: In our pluralistic and often secular age, Hebrews reminds believers of the uniqueness of Christ and the unshakeable nature of the kingdom he inaugurates. It challenges readers to anchor their identity, hope, and endurance in Jesus, who is the same yesterday, today, and forever (Heb. 13:8).

Liturgical and Devotional Value: Passages such as Hebrews 4:14–16 and 10:19–25 have long served as foundations for Christian worship and spiritual confidence. The epistle encourages believers to draw near to God with boldness, trusting in the sufficiency of Christ's intercession.

Throughout this textbook, we will approach Hebrews critically and pastorally — attending both to its historical context and its enduring voice for the church today. By exploring the letter's structure, theology, and rhetorical strategies, we hope to hear anew its call to "run with perseverance the race marked out for us" (Heb. 12:1). Hebrews is not merely an ancient sermon to a forgotten community; it is a living word that continues to challenge, comfort, and commission followers of Jesus Christ.

Chapter 2
Historical Context and Background

The Epistle to the Hebrews emerges from a complex and dynamic intersection of religious traditions, cultural influences, and socio-political pressures. It is not an abstract theological treatise but a deeply contextual document, shaped by the lived realities of its audience—likely a group of Jewish Christians or God-fearing Gentiles immersed in Jewish tradition, yet facing the disorienting challenges of marginalization and religious transformation. To grasp Hebrews' theological arguments and pastoral exhortations, one must attend carefully to the multifaceted matrix of Second Temple Judaism, Greco-Roman intellectual currents, and the identity struggles of early Christianity.

At the heart of Hebrews lies an intricate engagement with the theological grammar of Second Temple Judaism. The Jerusalem temple, with its Levitical priesthood and elaborate sacrificial system, provided not only the ritual framework for worship but also a cosmological and covenantal lens through which ancient Jews understood their relationship with God. The Day of Atonement, as the liturgical centerpiece of the Jewish calendar, encapsulated the hope of purification, reconciliation, and divine access. Hebrews appropriates this cultic imagery with theological precision, reimagining Jesus as the ultimate high priest whose self-offering surpasses the limitations of the Levitical order. This move is neither allegorical nor dismissive; it reflects a profound theological reconfiguration wherein the categories of sacrifice and priesthood are fulfilled—not abolished—in Christ's heavenly ministry (cf. Heb. 4–10).

Crucial to this reinterpretation is Hebrews' use of Scripture, particularly the Septuagint—the Greek translation of the Hebrew Bible. The epistle's reliance on texts such as Psalm 110, Exodus 25–28, and Jeremiah 31 is not proof-texting but a hermeneutical strategy to embed Jesus within the covenantal narrative of Israel. Hebrews reads the story of Israel not as superseded but as brought to eschatological fulfillment in Christ. The new covenant does not negate the old but brings to fruition its deepest promises. Jesus is presented not merely as a continuation of the covenantal line but as its climactic realization—the Son who mediates a better covenant founded on better promises (Heb. 8:6). This approach reflects an early Christian pattern of typological interpretation, whereby historical and liturgical elements are seen as anticipatory shadows of Christ's definitive work.

Moreover, the epistle is acutely aware of the eschatological hopes that permeated first-century Judaism. Apocalyptic literature of the period—from the Dead Sea Scrolls to 1 Enoch—testifies to a widespread longing for divine intervention, messianic deliverance, and cosmic renewal. Hebrews speaks into this atmosphere of expectation by presenting Jesus as both the awaited Davidic king and the eschatological high priest who has entered the heavenly sanctuary once for all (Heb. 9:11–12). His exaltation at the right hand of God is not simply a reward for obedience but a theological assertion of inaugurated eschatology: the future has broken into the present, and the heavenly reality now defines the true locus of worship.

Simultaneously, the epistle reflects the intellectual sophistication of the Hellenistic world. Its elegant Greek prose and rhetorical coherence suggest an author steeped in Greco-Roman paideia. Scholars have noted affinities with Middle Platonic thought, particularly in the epistle's contrast between temporal, earthly copies and eternal, heavenly realities (cf. Heb. 8:5; 9:23). However, Hebrews does not capitulate to dualism; rather, it adapts prevailing philosophical idioms to reinforce a Jewish theological vision. The heavenly tabernacle is not an escape from materiality but the true locus of divine presence, of which the earthly sanctuary was a divinely ordained symbol. In this way, Hebrews exemplifies the early Christian capacity to engage critically and constructively with surrounding philosophical discourse.

The socio-political context of Hebrews further illuminates its urgency. Though the epistle does not explicitly refer to imperial persecution, it testifies to a community experiencing ostracism, loss of property, and public shame (Heb. 10:32–34). This pressure likely stemmed from multiple fronts: separation from the synagogue, suspicion from Roman authorities, and estrangement from former networks of social and economic support. The pastoral tenor of the epistle—its repeated calls to perseverance, its warnings against apostasy, and its appeal to Christ's own suffering—suggests a congregation on the brink of spiritual fatigue. Hebrews responds not with triumphalism but with a theology of endurance rooted in the fidelity of Jesus, the pioneer and perfecter of faith (Heb. 12:2).

Against this backdrop, Hebrews also reveals the contested and transitional nature of early Christian identity. The boundary lines between Jews and Christ-followers were not yet clearly drawn. Indeed, many early believers would have continued to participate in synagogue life, observe Jewish customs, and self-identify within the broader framework of Jewish piety. Hebrews stands at the threshold of a new theological horizon. It affirms Israel's sacred story while insisting that this story reaches its goal in the risen Christ. The claim that the old covenant is "obsolete" (Heb. 8:13) must be understood as a declaration of fulfillment rather than repudiation. What is surpassed is not the truth of Israel's covenantal history but its provisional and anticipatory forms.

This theological transition extends to ecclesial and liturgical self-understanding. Whether the Jerusalem temple was still standing or had recently fallen, Hebrews challenges its readers to shift their focus from earthly rituals to the heavenly liturgy inaugurated by Christ. Access to God is no longer mediated through Levitical priests but through the exalted Son, who intercedes in the true sanctuary. This reorientation represents a monumental shift in the conceptualization of sacred space, sacred time, and priestly authority. It marks the movement from a religion of inherited forms to one of eschatological reality—a move that would define much of subsequent Christian theology.

In conclusion, Hebrews is a masterful synthesis of theological tradition, cultural engagement, and pastoral exhortation. It draws from the deep wells of Jewish covenantal theology, engages the conceptual resources of Hellenistic philosophy, and addresses the existential concerns of a beleaguered community. Its call to faithfulness is neither nostalgic nor escapist but rooted in the enduring reality of Christ's heavenly priesthood. In situating the Christ event within the grand arc of redemptive history and cosmic reality, Hebrews offers a compelling vision of Christian identity—one that is both deeply rooted and radically reoriented in the person and work of Jesus Christ.

Chapter 3
Authorship

The Epistle to the Hebrews is the only substantial early Christian text included in the New Testament whose author is entirely anonymous. Unlike Paul's letters, it begins with no greeting, no personal signature, and no direct claim of authority. Yet despite this silence, it found a secure place in the Christian canon. From the second century to the present, readers have debated who could have written such a rhetorically polished, theologically profound, and scripturally rich work. The question of authorship, while historically elusive, is not incidental. It intersects with larger questions about authority, tradition, and how the early church discerned which texts bore enduring witness to the gospel.

By the late second century, the name of Paul had become closely associated with Hebrews, especially in Alexandrian circles. Some writers, like Clement of Alexandria fully endorsed Pauline authorship and even suggested that Paul had omitted his name to avoid offending Jewish readers. Others, like Origen, expressed uncertainty; still others proposed entirely different figures. In Hebrews' case, its early inclusion in Greek collections of Pauline letters likely aided its recognition and use in churches. Though anonymous, Hebrews gained credibility in part through its proximity to the Pauline tradition, which helped anchor it within apostolic authority and opened the way for its eventual canonization.

Modern scholarship overwhelmingly rejects Pauline authorship on linguistic and theological grounds. The Greek of Hebrews is more elegant and literary than Paul's often rugged prose. The argumentation is highly structured, the vocabulary distinctive, and the theological emphases — particularly the focus on Jesus' heavenly priesthood — are without parallel in Paul's undisputed letters. Moreover, the author acknowledges having received the gospel through others (Heb. 2:3), a claim that seems at odds with Paul's insistence on receiving it by direct revelation (Gal. 1:12). These factors together have led scholars to seek other candidates for authorship.

Several proposals have been offered, each attempting to account for the letter's intellectual sophistication and theological depth. Barnabas, an early Christian leader and companion of Paul, has been suggested as a possibility. Apollos, an eloquent Alexandrian described in Acts as "mighty in the Scriptures," remains a popular choice, especially given the letter's rhetorical polish and rich use of the Old Testament. Others have proposed Luke, noting some stylistic similarities, or Priscilla, whose prominence in the early church and omission from the letter's tradition could be explained by gender biases. Yet none of these theories has achieved widespread consensus.

Despite its anonymity, Hebrews exerted considerable influence in the early church. Its depiction of Christ as High Priest, its sophisticated interpretation of Scripture, and its exhortations to perseverance resonated with Christian communities facing social and theological pressures. If authorship was uncertain, the power of the letter's theology was not. Still, Hebrews' association with Paul—however cautious—helped position it within the developing canon and lent it an apostolic prestige that bolstered its reception.

In the end, the anonymity of Hebrews serves to underscore the message it proclaims. The letter, like Melchizedek, appears without genealogy, its authority grounded not in the name of its human author but in the transcendent word it bears. Hebrews invites its readers to shift their focus from questions of provenance to the one in whom God has spoken fully and finally: Jesus Christ, the Son.

Chapter 4
Audience and Occasion

If authorship is one of the enduring mysteries of Hebrews, the identity of its audience is scarcely less elusive. The letter — or sermon, as some have called it — offers no direct address, no specific location, and no obvious historical markers. Yet the epistle communicates with unmistakable pastoral urgency, addressing a community under pressure, at risk of spiritual drift, and in need of exhortation to persevere. Who were these people? And what circumstances provoked such a sustained theological and rhetorical response?

The most common assumption is that the audience was composed of Jewish Christians. The content of Hebrews supports this: the dense engagement with the Hebrew Scriptures, the familiarity with Levitical rituals and covenantal categories, and the sustained focus on priesthood, sacrifice, and the tabernacle all point in this direction. But "Jewish Christian" is a broad and contested label. It may refer to ethnically Jewish believers in Jesus, to Gentiles participating in Jewish-Christian communities, or to Christians deeply rooted in Israel's Scriptures and cultic imagination. Hebrews never uses the word "Jew," and its argument is constructed not in ethnic but theological terms. It is better, then, to think of the audience as a group of Christ-followers steeped in the symbolic and scriptural world of Second Temple Judaism—whether by birth, association, or education.

The social situation of the audience can be inferred from several clues within the text. Hebrews 10:32–34 refers to a "former time" when the community endured persecution, public shaming, and the plundering of their possessions. These events seem to be in the past, but their memory still informs the present. The letter repeatedly warns against falling away and urges the readers to "hold fast" (4:14; 10:23). This suggests not only external pressure but internal fatigue. The issue may not be overt rejection of Christ, but a gradual erosion of faith, perhaps due to weariness, disillusionment, or social isolation.

Some scholars have speculated that the audience was facing the temptation to return to Judaism or to seek shelter within more socially acceptable religious forms. This reading, though plausible, risks oversimplifying both Judaism and early Christianity. The idea of "going back" assumes a clear line of departure, when in fact many early believers may have seen themselves as remaining within the bounds of Jewish covenantal life even as they followed Jesus as Messiah. The author of Hebrews does not accuse the audience of abandoning Judaism but instead calls them to see that the promises of the Scriptures have been fulfilled in Christ. The concern is not religious identity per se, but faithfulness to the revealed word of God in the Son.

The geographic setting of the audience remains uncertain. Rome is a leading possibility, partly based on the mention of "those from Italy" in the closing greeting (13:24). The first-century Roman church included both Jewish and Gentile members, and it experienced periodic tensions as well as imperial scrutiny, especially under Claudius and Nero. A Roman context could explain both the persecution allusions and the educated rhetorical style of the letter. Others have proposed Jerusalem, Alexandria, or a diaspora community in Asia Minor, but no location fits definitively. Ultimately, the epistle's concerns are not tied to one local situation but resonate with the broader condition of early Christian communities negotiating identity, suffering, and hope.

What occasioned the letter? Most interpreters agree that the community was not in open rebellion but in danger of passive neglect—what Hebrews calls "drifting away" (2:1) or developing "sluggishness" (5:11). The recurring warnings against apostasy are severe, but they function as part of a pastoral strategy: not condemnation, but provocation toward endurance. The letter's rhetorical rhythm alternates between theological exposition and exhortation, creating a pattern designed to stir memory, rekindle hope, and re-anchor faith. The author, whoever they were, writes not as a detached theologian but as a preacher and pastor deeply invested in the spiritual perseverance of the hearers.

Hebrews speaks to a community at a crossroads—not simply doctrinally, but existentially. Will they endure, or will they retreat? Will they respond to the word of God spoken "in these last days" in the Son, or will they drift toward indifference? The letter's concern is not merely with correct belief but with the endurance of hope and the constancy of obedience. Its vision of Christ enthroned, interceding, and returning becomes both the anchor and the motivation for continuing in faith.

Though their precise identity may remain unknown, the audience of Hebrews emerges as a community very much like the church in many times and places: discouraged, tempted, spiritually exhausted, and in need of a renewed vision of who Jesus is and why he matters. The occasion for the letter, then, is nothing less than the enduring human struggle to remain faithful in a world that presses for compromise. Hebrews addresses that struggle not by minimizing it, but by lifting the eyes of the weary to a better promise, a better priest, and a better hope.

Chapter 5
Structure, Genre, and Rhetoric

Few New Testament writings are as rhetorically polished and structurally intricate as Hebrews. Its careful progression of thought, its weaving of scriptural exposition and exhortation, and its high literary style make it stand apart from other epistles. But these same features have made it difficult to classify. Is Hebrews a letter? A theological treatise? A sermon? The question of genre is more than an academic exercise; it shapes how we read the work and understand its purpose.

Although it closes with epistolary conventions — a reference to Timothy, a final greeting, and a blessing — the bulk of Hebrews lacks the opening structure of a typical Greco-Roman letter. There is no sender or recipient identified, no thanksgiving or prayer, and no initial benediction. These omissions have led many scholars to argue that Hebrews is not really a letter but something closer to a homily or sermon. Indeed, the author refers to it as a "word of exhortation" (13:22), a phrase used elsewhere in the New Testament to describe public preaching (cf. Acts 13:15).

This has led to the widespread view that Hebrews is best read as a written sermon — a piece of oral rhetoric later put into literary form. Its structure supports this reading: rather than a series of loosely connected teachings, Hebrews unfolds a unified and progressive argument. The theological exposition builds steadily—from the exaltation of the Son in chapter 1 to the call for perseverance in the face of suffering in chapter 12—interspersed with strategically placed warning passages. These rhetorical shifts from exposition to exhortation function much like the turns in a well-crafted sermon: theology in the service of formation.

One of the most compelling developments in recent scholarship has come from Gabriella Gelardini, who has argued that Hebrews should be understood as a synagogue homily, possibly preached for the ninth of Av (*Tisha B'Av*)—the annual day of mourning in the Jewish calendar that commemorated the destruction of the temple. In this reading, the entire structure and theological emphasis of Hebrews cohere around themes of temple loss, covenant disruption, and the hope of divine restoration.

Gelardini's argument builds on several observations. First, the text is deeply concerned with the tabernacle, the priesthood, and the sacrificial system—not in abstract terms but as institutions now surpassed and fulfilled. Second, the rhetorical function of Hebrews mirrors that of post-70 Jewish homilies, which sought to interpret the meaning of the temple's destruction in theological terms. In this light, Hebrews' exposition of a heavenly sanctuary and a superior priesthood in Christ may reflect an effort to reframe temple loss not as tragedy but as theological transition.

Reading Hebrews as a Tisha B'Av homily also casts new light on its tone and urgency. The text does not simply explain Christ's priesthood; it laments what has been lost and announces what has now been inaugurated. Its warnings are not abstract theological constructs but part of a liturgical strategy designed to awaken memory and summon perseverance. Gelardini's proposal does not rule out Christian authorship or audience; rather, it recognizes the extent to which Hebrews is embedded in a Jewish rhetorical and homiletical world, employing the structures and conventions of synagogue preaching to proclaim Jesus as the culmination of Israel's story.

More broadly, Hebrews also reflects the influence of Greco-Roman rhetoric, particularly in its use of synkrisis (comparison), enthymeme (implied argument), and amplification. The contrast between the earthly and the heavenly, the old and the new, the shadow and the reality — these are not merely theological contrasts but carefully crafted rhetorical devices. The author is not just informing the audience but persuading them, moving them emotionally and intellectually toward renewed conviction.

The overall structure of Hebrews remains a subject of debate, but most interpreters agree that the argument proceeds in concentric layers, with central theological themes introduced, expanded, and revisited in light of exhortation. Rather than a linear sequence of topics, the structure resembles a homiletical spiral, with each turn returning to core claims: the superiority of

Christ, the fulfillment of Scripture, and the necessity of perseverance.

To call Hebrews a sermon, then, is not to diminish its theological depth but to acknowledge its liturgical function. It is theology delivered with pastoral urgency, scripture interpreted for the sake of endurance, and rhetoric crafted for the transformation of its hearers. Whether preached in a synagogue or written for a house church, Hebrews seeks not only to inform but to awaken, exhort, and sustain. Its genre is shaped by its goal: to keep the weary faithful by showing them the glory of Christ.

Chapter 6
Theological Themes
and the Use of the Old Testament

Few writings in the New Testament rival Hebrews in theological ambition. With soaring Christological claims, a reimagined vision of covenant and worship, and sustained exhortation to perseverance, Hebrews functions both as doctrinal instruction and pastoral exhortation. But its theology does not arise abstractly; it is forged through Scripture. The Old Testament is not merely cited in Hebrews — it is inhabited, interpreted, and fulfilled. Theology in Hebrews is always scriptural theology, shaped through the lens of Christ.

At the center of Hebrews stands a majestic Christology. The Son is "the radiance of God's glory and the exact imprint of his being" (1:3), exalted above angels, enthroned at the right hand of God, and declared both King and Priest. No other New Testament text draws so directly and systematically on the royal and priestly dimensions of Jesus' identity. Christ is not only the final word of God's revelation but also the one who mediates between God and humanity. He is the faithful high priest who has passed through the heavens, the Son made perfect through suffering, the guarantor of a better covenant. The argument is not only ontological — who Jesus is — but also vocational — what Jesus does: interceding, cleansing, reigning.

This Christology is inseparable from Hebrews' portrayal of covenant and worship. The letter contrasts the old and new covenants not to disparage the former, but to show its fulfillment. The tabernacle, the sacrificial system, the Levitical priesthood — all served as shadows or anticipations of the heavenly realities now inaugurated through Christ. The central claim is not that Israel's institutions were defective, but that they were preparatory. The new covenant, introduced through the citation of Jeremiah 31 (Heb. 8:8–12), brings internal transformation and direct access to God. Christ, having entered the heavenly sanctuary "once for all," has accomplished what the repetitive sacrifices of the old order could not: full and final atonement.

Closely tied to this covenantal theology is Hebrews' vision of salvation and perseverance. Salvation is not reduced to a singular event or moment of belief; it is a dynamic process grounded in Christ's priestly work and extending through the believer's faithful response. Hebrews repeatedly warns against the danger of "falling away" and urges its audience to "hold fast" to their confession. Faith is not merely cognitive assent but persevering trust. This is perhaps most memorably articulated in Hebrews 11, where the author surveys Israel's past as a gallery of faithful endurance: from Abel to Moses, from Rahab to unnamed martyrs, faith is the through-line of salvation history.

Running throughout all of this is Hebrews' distinctive use of the Old Testament. No New Testament writing quotes Scripture more densely or builds its argument more completely on scriptural interpretation. The text leans heavily on the Greek Septuagint, often citing passages in ways that differ from the Hebrew Masoretic tradition. This is not a casual borrowing of prooftexts, but a theologically driven reading strategy. Hebrews treats the Psalms, the Torah, and the Prophets not as static texts but as living oracles — words spoken not only in the past, but in the present, and ultimately by God himself.

Perhaps most striking is the way Hebrews uses Psalm 110, which stands at the very center of the letter's theological argument. Psalm 110:1 ("Sit at my right hand until I make your enemies your footstool") was widely cited in early Christian writings to affirm Christ's exaltation, but Hebrews alone among New Testament texts makes extensive use of Psalm 110:4: "You are a priest forever, according to the order of Melchizedek." These two verses form the dual spine of Hebrews' portrait of Christ: enthroned Son and eternal High Priest. Psalm 110:1 grounds Jesus' heavenly session — his exaltation and reign at God's right hand — while Psalm 110:4 establishes the typological foundation for a non-Levitical priesthood, rooted not in genealogy but in divine appointment. By linking these two verses, Hebrews constructs a uniquely royal-priestly Christology that shapes the entire letter. The Son is not only reigning but interceding, not only glorified but mediating a better covenant through his own self-offering.

Perhaps even more remarkable is that God is consistently portrayed as the speaker of Scripture. Whether the text quotes David, Moses, or the prophets, Hebrews attributes their words to God or to the Holy Spirit: "as the Holy Spirit says…" (3:7). Scripture is not treated as a historical artifact but as the living, divine voice. This reflects the opening claim of the letter — that God has spoken "in many times and in many ways" through the prophets, but now definitively "in the Son" (1:1–2). The continuity between the old and new revelations is not broken but fulfilled.

In this way, Hebrews offers a distinct hermeneutic: Christ is the key to reading Scripture, and Scripture is the means of understanding Christ. Typology — especially the pattern of promise and fulfillment — governs much of the interpretation. The tabernacle is a type of the heavenly sanctuary; the priesthood a foreshadowing of Christ's intercession; the wilderness generation a mirror of the community's own precarious moment. The goal is not to abandon the Hebrews Scriptures, but to see them new eyes, reoriented around the reality to which they point.

Theologically rich and textually saturated, Hebrews models a form of biblical interpretation that is both reverent and radical. It calls its readers to faith not on the basis of novelty, but fulfillment; not through innovation, but through realization. Its vision is one of continuity transformed: the promises to the ancestors have not been revoked—they have been realized in a better priest, a better covenant, and a better hope.

Chapter 7
God's Climactic Word
The Son Superior to Angels
(Hebrews 1:1–2:4)

The opening movement of Hebrews begins not with argument but with proclamation. There is no greeting, no thanksgiving, no mention of the author or recipients. Instead, the epistle begins like a sermon: "Long ago, God spoke to our ancestors in many and various ways by the prophets, but in these last days he has spoken to us by a Son" (1:1–2). The contrast is not between false and true revelation, but between partial and final. The God who spoke is the same; what has changed is the clarity, fullness, and agency of that speech.

This opening sentence sets the theological trajectory for the entire epistle. Revelation is neither abstract nor propositional—it is personal. God has spoken "by a Son," who is then described in a sevenfold crescendo: heir of all things, agent of creation, radiance of God's glory, exact imprint of God's being, sustainer of all things, the one who made purification for sins, and the one now seated at God's right hand. In these few verses, the author brings together cosmology, Christology, atonement, and enthronement. The Son is not simply another prophet; he is the goal and agent of all that God has done.

What follows in 1:5–14 is a carefully structured series of scriptural quotations, all drawn from the Septuagint and arranged to support the Son's superiority to the angels. The use of catenae—chains of Scripture—was a common technique in Jewish preaching, and here it serves both a theological and rhetorical function. The Son is described in contrast to angels not because the audience was necessarily tempted to worship angels, but because the exaltation of the Son must be grounded in Scripture, and angels provide a fitting point of contrast. They are honored messengers; the Son is the enthroned King.

Several of the texts cited are royal psalms, reinterpreted in light of Jesus' identity. Psalm 2:7 ("You are my Son; today I have begotten you") and 2 Samuel 7:14 ("I will be his father, and he will be my son") anchor the Sonship motif in the Davidic tradition. Psalm 45:6–7 and Psalm 102:25–27 are applied to the Son to underscore his divine status, eternal rule, and role in creation. These citations are not mined for prooftexts but carefully arranged to portray the Son as divine, eternal, sovereign, and unique—set apart even from the heavenly host.

The climax comes in the final citation of the chapter, Psalm 110:1: "Sit at my right hand until I make your enemies a footstool for your feet." This verse, as noted in the previous chapter, was widely cited in early Christianity and is foundational for Hebrews. It affirms not only Christ's exaltation but also his enthronement, theologically grounding the claim that Jesus now reigns with God, having completed the priestly work of purification. Though Hebrews will not explore the priestly dimension of this enthronement until later chapters, the seeds are sown here.

Chapter 2 opens with a shift in tone. The lofty Christological exposition gives way to the first of several warnings in Hebrews. "Therefore we must pay greater attention to what we have heard, so that we do not drift away" (2:1). The danger is not active rebellion but passive neglect. Just as Israel once failed to heed the word spoken through angels (a reference to the tradition that the law was mediated by angels), so the community now faces the danger of failing to heed the word spoken through the Son.

This warning is framed not only by fear of judgment, but by the weight of the gospel's divine validation. The message was declared by the Lord, attested by eyewitnesses, and confirmed by God through "signs and wonders and various miracles, and by gifts of the Holy Spirit" (2:3-4). In this way, the early community's charismatic experience becomes part of the theological appeal. The past must not be forgotten; it is the evidence that God has spoken decisively, and to neglect that word is to risk losing everything.

This first major section of Hebrews thus establishes both the identity of the Son and the urgency of faith. The one who now reigns is no mere teacher or messenger but the radiant image of God and the heir of all things. The Scriptures testify to his exalted status, and the church's experience confirms the message. The proper response is not speculation but attention — not distraction, but perseverance. The grandeur of the Son is not a theological ornament; it is the basis for faithfulness in a difficult world.

Excursus: Psalm 110:1 in Early Christianity

Psalm 110:1 — "The Lord said to my Lord, 'Sit at my right hand until I make your enemies your footstool'" — emerges as one of the most frequently cited and theologically significant Old Testament texts in the New Testament. Its appearance in Hebrews 1:13, concluding a majestic chain of scriptural quotations exalting the Son above the angels, reflects a broader early Christian pattern: Psalm 110:1 was central to the way the early church articulated the identity and exaltation of Jesus.

In its original context, Psalm 110 was likely a royal psalm, possibly composed for a coronation or enthronement ceremony. The psalmist (perhaps David) envisions a divine utterance to the newly installed king, addressed with the exalted title "my Lord." The imagery of sitting at God's right hand conveyed a position of supreme honor, authority, and delegated sovereignty. The verse also promises divine victory over the king's enemies, suggesting a future-oriented hope in the power and security of the Davidic throne.

Early Christians, particularly those steeped in the Septuagint (LXX), recognized in Psalm 110:1 a prophetic foreshadowing of Jesus' resurrection and exaltation. The text's appeal lay not only in its royal themes but in its implied multiplicity of divine persons: "The Lord said to my Lord." Jesus himself famously referenced the verse in his debates with religious leaders

(Mark 12:35–37; cf. Matt 22:41–46; Luke 20:41–44), challenging conventional understandings of the Messiah as merely David's son. For Jesus and the early church, Psalm 110:1 suggested a messianic figure greater than David—one who shares in divine authority.

The verse became foundational in apostolic preaching. Peter quotes it in his Pentecost sermon in Acts 2:34–35, using it to declare that God has made Jesus "both Lord and Christ." Paul alludes to its themes of enthronement and subjugation in 1 Corinthians 15:25 and Ephesians 1:20–22. The image of Jesus seated at God's right hand became a central affirmation in the early church's confession and creeds, emphasizing both the triumph of the resurrection and the ongoing heavenly reign of Christ.

Hebrews adopts this tradition but intensifies it. By placing Psalm 110:1 at the climax of a series of exalted declarations about the Son (Heb. 1:13), the author signals that Christ's enthronement is not merely honorary—it is ontological. Jesus is not only the exalted messianic king but the divine Son who shares in the very nature of God (Heb. 1:3). The citation sets the stage for the later use of Psalm 110:4, which introduces the unique priesthood of Christ "according to the order of Melchizedek." Together, Psalm 110:1 and 110:4 form the backbone of Hebrews' royal-priestly Christology.

The widespread and enduring use of Psalm 110:1 in early Christianity underscores its theological power. It allowed the church to articulate Jesus' exaltation in continuity with Israel's Scriptures, to speak of his present lordship and heavenly session, and to anticipate his final victory over all powers. In Hebrews, as in the wider New Testament, Psalm 110:1 is not simply a prooftext but a cornerstone for understanding who Jesus is and where he now reigns.

Chapter 8
A Faithful and Merciful High Priest
(Hebrews 2:5–4:13)

Having exalted the Son above the angels, the author of Hebrews now pivots toward what initially seems a reversal: the Son's identification with humanity in suffering and death. But this is no contradiction. The very exaltation of the Son depends on his solidarity with those he came to save. It is not despite his humanity but through it that he becomes "a merciful and faithful high priest" (2:17). Hebrews 2:5–4:13 begins to lay the theological groundwork for this priesthood — a theme that will dominate the chapters to come.

The section opens with a citation of Psalm 8, a hymn celebrating the honor bestowed on humanity within creation. "What are human beings that you are mindful of them...?" (2:6). In its original context, Psalm 8 reflects on human frailty and divine generosity. Hebrews, however, reads the psalm christologically. The subject is not humanity in general, but the Son, who was for a little while "lower than the angels" and now "crowned with glory and honor because of the suffering of death" (2:9). This re-reading is typological: Jesus, as the representative human, fulfills the vocation described in the psalm — ruling over the world, not by avoiding suffering, but by entering it fully.

This theme of solidarity through suffering continues through the rest of chapter 2. The incarnation is described not simply as a metaphysical event but as an act of redemptive identification. "Since the children share flesh and blood, he himself likewise shared the same things" (2:14). The Son became like his brothers and sisters "in every respect" so that he might destroy the power of death and liberate those enslaved by fear. Crucially, this is not incidental to his mission but essential: he had to become like them in order to represent them before God. Priesthood here is not defined institutionally but relationally. It arises from shared experience, not tribal lineage.

The transition to chapter 3 marks a new stage in the argument, but the logic continues. The audience is now directly addressed as "holy partners in a heavenly calling" (3:1), invited to "consider Jesus, the apostle and high priest of our confession." The word *apostle* — used uniquely here in the New Testament — emphasizes Jesus' role as one sent from God, while *high priest* will anchor the next major sections of the epistle. The comparison that follows, between Jesus and Moses, highlights both continuity and contrast. Moses was faithful "in all his house" as a servant; Jesus is faithful as a Son over the house. The image evokes not competition but succession — Jesus brings to fulfillment what Moses anticipated.

At this point the letter takes a sharp exhortational turn. Drawing on Psalm 95, the author warns the audience not to harden their hearts as the wilderness generation did. The theological focus has not shifted; it has intensified. The contrast is no longer only between Jesus and the angels or Moses, but between faithful and unfaithful response. The generation that perished in the wilderness had received the promises and seen God's works, but they failed to enter God's "rest" because of unbelief.

This theme of "rest" becomes a key motif in chapter 4. The promise still stands, the author insists, and the people of God are still being invited to enter it. But entry is not automatic. It requires attentiveness, perseverance, and faith. Just as the Word once came to Israel in the past so now it comes to Hebrews' audience—and it demands response. Hebrews 4:12–13 delivers a sobering conclusion: "Indeed, the word of God is living and active... discerning the thoughts and intentions of the heart." God's speech is not safely external; it penetrates to the core of the human person and reveals what is truly there.

In this section, we begin to see how Christ's priesthood emerges not from distance but from proximity. He is not aloof from human weakness but has experienced it—suffering, temptation, mortality. This shared experience gives depth to his intercession and authenticity to his advocacy. The high priest of Hebrews is not the idealized figure of distant cultic ritual but the embodied, suffering, and exalted Son who knows what it is to be human. The pastoral logic is clear: if this is the one who represents us before God, then we can draw near with confidence.

Excursus: The "Word of God" in Hebrews

Among the many theological themes woven throughout the Epistle to the Hebrews, few are as rich and multilayered as its portrayal of the "word of God." Unlike some New Testament texts where the phrase may refer narrowly to the written Scriptures or apostolic preaching, Hebrews employs the concept more dynamically and expansively. In Hebrews, the word of God is living, active, divine, and personal — it is God's self-communication that both discloses and accomplishes divine purposes.

The epistle opens with a high Christological claim that is also a statement about divine speech: "In many times and in many ways God spoke to our ancestors by the prophets, but in these last days he has spoken to us by a Son..." (Heb. 1:1-2). Here, the "word" is not merely propositional or textual but incarnational. Jesus himself is the ultimate word of God — the climactic act of revelation. This sets the tone for Hebrews' understanding of divine communication: God's word is not static; it culminates in a person who embodies and fulfills everything previously spoken.

Yet Hebrews also continues to speak of the "word of God" in ways that include Scripture, exhortation, and divine agency. Hebrews 3:7 introduces a citation of Psalm 95 with the formula, "As the Holy Spirit says," signaling that Scripture remains an active, divine voice. This is not merely a record of what God once said but an expression of what God is still saying through the Spirit. The Scriptures, for Hebrews, are not historical artifacts; they are a living medium of divine speech that addresses the present community.

This same dynamism appears in one of Hebrews' most quoted verses: "The word of God is living and active, sharper than any two-edged sword, piercing to the division of soul and spirit... and discerning the thoughts and intentions of the heart" (Heb. 4:12). Here, the word of God functions almost as an agent of judgment, penetrating the human conscience and exposing what lies hidden. The description suggests not only the convicting power of Scripture but the broader, divine speech that confronts the community with truth and demands a response. It also reinforces that God's word is inseparable from God's presence — powerful, penetrating, and unescapable.

The connection between the word and covenant also becomes apparent in Hebrews 8. As the author quotes Jeremiah 31:31–34 at length, he underscores a new covenant defined by internalized divine instruction: "I will put my laws in their minds and write them on their hearts" (Heb. 8:10). In contrast to the written laws mediated externally through Moses, the new covenant involves God's word written directly on the heart. This internalization represents a movement from command to transformation — from obligation to relationship. The word of God, in this new covenantal frame, is not only a standard but an implanted power that enables obedience and intimacy with God.

Thus, throughout Hebrews, the word of God functions in several interrelated ways:

As Revelation: God has spoken fully and finally in the Son, Jesus Christ (1:1–2).

As Scripture: The Spirit continues to speak through Israel's Scriptures, now interpreted in light of Christ (3:7; 4:7; 10:15).

As Power: The word is active, discerning, and capable of cutting to the heart (4:12).

As Covenant: God's laws are written on the hearts of believers as part of the new covenant, signifying internal transformation (8:10).

These uses resist compartmentalization. Instead, Hebrews presents a unified vision in which the word of God is coherent with the person of Christ, the witness of Scripture, and the inner working of the Spirit. It is not surprising, then, that the epistle itself—sometimes called a "word of exhortation" (13:22)—participates in this divine speech. As a sermon or homily, Hebrews speaks not only about the word of God but also as a medium through which it continues to be heard.

In this light, to encounter the word of God in Hebrews is not merely to receive information or instruction but to stand before a speaking, discerning, and transformative God. The community is called not just to listen passively but to respond with obedience, perseverance, and awe.

Chapter 9
A Priest Forever
(Hebrews 4:14–7:28)

The brief reference to Jesus as high priest in earlier chapters now expands into Hebrews' central theological theme: the eternal priesthood of Christ. Beginning in 4:14, the author of Hebrews invites the audience to draw near to God, not through fear or ritual mediation, but through the gracious intercession of a high priest who is both exalted and empathetic. This priesthood is not inherited through Levitical descent but established by divine oath — "according to the order of Melchizedek." Hebrews 4:14–7:28 is the sustained theological meditation that unpacks what this means.

The section opens with an exhortation: "Let us hold fast to our confession" (4:14). This call is grounded in the identity of Jesus as "a great high priest who has passed through the heavens." Unlike the Levitical priests who ministered in an earthly sanctuary, Jesus has entered the heavenly one. Yet his exaltation does not distance him from human experience. On the contrary, "we do not have a high priest who is unable to sympathize with our weaknesses," for he has been tested in every respect, "yet without sin" (4:15). The priesthood of Christ brings together transcendence and compassion, exaltation and solidarity. As a result, believers are invited to approach the throne of grace with boldness.

Chapter 5 further develops the concept of priesthood, first by articulating the qualifications for a high priest: chosen from among the people, appointed to represent them before God, and able to deal gently with the ignorant and wayward. The author then applies these criteria to Christ, noting that he "did not glorify himself" to become a priest, but was appointed by God. Two scriptural citations confirm this: Psalm 2:7 ("You are my Son…") and Psalm 110:4 ("You are a priest forever according to the order of Melchizedek"). These verses together establish both divine sonship and divine appointment—core pillars of Hebrews' Christology.

But how does Melchizedek function in this argument? Mentioned only briefly in Genesis 14 as the king of Salem and priest of God Most High, Melchizedek blesses Abram and receives tithes from him. Psalm 110 later references him as the model for an eternal priesthood. Hebrews draws out the theological implications of this shadowy figure: Melchizedek appears without genealogy, without recorded beginning or end, making him a fitting type of the eternal Christ. He is both king and priest, combining two roles that were normally separate in Israelite tradition. By linking Jesus to Melchizedek rather than to Levi or Aaron, Hebrews creates space for a priesthood that is non-Levitical, non-hereditary, and superior.

Chapter 7 is devoted almost entirely to Melchizedek and the implications of his priesthood. The argument is built on typology: Melchizedek is "made like the Son of God," not the other way around. His priesthood is prior to and greater than the Levitical one because even Abraham, the ancestor of Levi, offered tithes to him and received a blessing from him. In the logic of Hebrews, the greater blesses the lesser. Therefore, if perfection had come through the Levitical priesthood, "what further need would there have been to speak of another priest... according to the order of Melchizedek?" (7:11).

The contrast becomes sharper as the chapter progresses. The Levitical priesthood was based on legal requirement and physical descent; Christ's priesthood is based on the power of an indestructible life. The former involved many priests, subject to death and succession; the latter is held permanently by one who "always lives to make intercession" (7:25). The Levitical priests offered sacrifices repeatedly; Christ offers himself once for all. The cumulative effect is to present Jesus as the final and perfect high priest, whose priesthood does not depend on ancestry but on divine appointment and eternal efficacy.

Hebrews 7:26–28 summarizes the argument with elevated language: "holy, blameless, undefiled, separated from sinners, and exalted above the heavens." This high priest does not need to offer sacrifices day after day. He offered himself once, and that once is enough. His priesthood is not only eternal but sufficient. In contrast to the weakness of the law, "the word of the oath"—again citing Psalm 110—has appointed the Son, "who has been made perfect forever."

At the heart of this section lies a redefinition of priesthood itself. It is no longer tied to cultic lineage or temple ritual but to divine election, moral perfection, and eternal intercession. Jesus' priesthood is not a temporary arrangement or a symbolic role. It is the theological centerpiece of how Hebrews understands salvation, access to God, and the unfolding of redemptive history.

For the hearers of Hebrews, this portrait of Christ as eternal priest is both a doctrinal anchor and a pastoral comfort. Their hope does not rest on institutional religion or earthly mediation but on a high priest who lives forever and never ceases to intercede for them. In Christ, the distance between heaven and earth has been bridged—not ritually but permanently, not symbolically but actually. And in that assurance, they are urged to persevere.

Excursus: Melchizedek in Ancient Jewish Literature

The figure of Melchizedek plays a pivotal role in the theological argument of Hebrews, particularly in chapter 7, where he is portrayed as a type of Christ— eternal, superior to the Levitical priesthood, and divinely appointed. However, Melchizedek's role in Hebrews is not an isolated innovation. The author draws upon, and likely expects familiarity with, broader traditions surrounding Melchizedek in Jewish interpretation and literature, where this enigmatic priest-king of Genesis 14 acquired rich symbolic significance.

In the biblical text of Genesis 14:18–20, Melchizedek appears abruptly in the narrative of Abram's military victory. He is introduced as "king of Salem" and "priest of God Most High" who blesses Abram and receives a tithe from him. The brevity of the account and the absence of genealogical or narrative background invited theological speculation in later Jewish interpretation. Psalm 110:4 would later elevate Melchizedek further: "You are a priest forever, according to the order of Melchizedek." Hebrews seizes on this combination of narrative obscurity and priestly status to construct a Christological type, but it was not the first to do so.

In Second Temple Judaism, Melchizedek appears in a variety of texts — some of them speculative, others highly exalted. Most notable among these are the texts found at Qumran and later rabbinic interpretations.

1. Melchizedek in Qumran Texts

The most significant Second Temple reinterpretation of Melchizedek comes from 11QMelchizedek (11Q13), a Dead Sea Scrolls fragment dated to the first century BCE. In this eschatological midrash, Melchizedek is portrayed not merely as a human priest but as a divine or semi-divine figure who functions as a heavenly deliverer. He is described using titles like "elohim" (God) and "judge," and he is expected to play a decisive role in the Day of Atonement at the end of days.

In this text, Melchizedek acts as a heavenly priestly figure who proclaims liberty to the captives, drawing from Leviticus 25 and Isaiah 52. He functions as a messianic agent of atonement and judgment, opposing the forces of Belial (evil) and presiding over God's final jubilee. This portrayal reveals that by the time Hebrews was written, Melchizedek had already been associated with eschatological hope and divine authority in some Jewish circles.

The author of Hebrews does not directly quote 11QMelchizedek but seems aware of this tradition. He echoes the idea of Melchizedek's heavenly origin, priestly status, and eschatological function, though he channels these attributes Christologically. In Hebrews, Christ — not Melchizedek — is the true eternal priest, but Melchizedek provides a pattern or archetype for understanding Jesus' unique priesthood.

2. Melchizedek in Philo

The Hellenistic Jewish philosopher Philo of Alexandria also comments on Melchizedek, though in a more allegorical mode. In *Legum Allegoriae* and *De Congressu Quaerendae Eruditionis Gratia*, Philo interprets Melchizedek as a symbol of reason or virtue, part of his broader allegorical approach to Scripture. Philo identifies Melchizedek with "logos" — the divine reason — and emphasizes his ethical and philosophical function.

While Philo's allegory differs from Hebrews' typology, both approaches treat Melchizedek as more than a historical figure. He is an interpretive key to something greater: for Philo, abstract wisdom; for Hebrews, the eternal priesthood of the exalted Christ.

3. Melchizedek in Rabbinic and Later Jewish Sources

In later rabbinic literature, Melchizedek is typically demystified. Some rabbinic texts associate Melchizedek with Shem, the son of Noah, thereby grounding him within the biblical genealogical tradition and removing the aura of mystery emphasized in earlier Jewish and Christian readings. This move may reflect a reaction against Christian claims, including those in Hebrews, which heavily invested Melchizedek with messianic and theological significance.

While rabbinic texts preserve a degree of respect for Melchizedek's priestly role, they often shift focus back to Abraham as the central patriarchal figure, thereby affirming Abrahamic and Levitical continuity over Melchizedekian innovation.

The Epistle to the Hebrews stands within a larger interpretive tradition that saw Melchizedek as more than a minor biblical character. Second Temple Jewish texts — especially 11QMelchizedek — show that Melchizedek had become a flexible symbol: a heavenly priest, a figure of righteousness, and a bearer of eschatological hope.

Hebrews adopts and transforms this tradition by locating its fulfillment in Christ. Rather than casting Jesus as Melchizedek, it presents Melchizedek as a type — a shadow — of the true high priest who is eternal not merely because of mysterious origins but because of divine appointment and resurrection power. In this way, Hebrews uses Melchizedek not as an end in himself, but as a means of illuminating the incomparable priesthood of Christ.

Chapter 10
The Mediator of a Better Covenant
(Hebrews 8:1–13)

Having firmly established Christ's priesthood as superior to the Levitical order, Hebrews now turns explicitly to the nature and implications of the "better covenant" inaugurated through Christ (Hebrews 8:6). The eighth chapter of Hebrews is concise yet pivotal, forming a bridge between the theological exposition of Christ's priesthood and the sacrificial imagery detailed in subsequent chapters. At its heart lies a profound reinterpretation of the ancient covenant promises in light of Jesus' heavenly ministry.

The author of Hebrews summarizes the preceding argument with clarity: "Now the main point of what we are saying is this: we do have such a high priest, who sat down at the right hand of the throne of the Majesty in heaven" (Heb. 8:1). This declaration succinctly encapsulates the entirety of Hebrews' Christological vision. Christ's seated posture symbolizes the completion and sufficiency of his priestly work, contrasting sharply with the perpetual standing and continuous sacrifices of Levitical priests. His heavenly enthronement signals that he ministers in "the true tabernacle set up by the Lord, not by a mere human being" (Heb. 8:2).

Hebrews draws upon imagery reminiscent of Platonic philosophy to differentiate sharply between earthly and heavenly realities. The earthly tabernacle, though divinely instructed and revered, is characterized explicitly as "a copy and shadow of what is in heaven" (Heb. 8:5). This notion reflects a worldview common among Hellenistic Jews, notably influenced by Middle Platonism, yet Hebrews employs it not to devalue the earthly sanctuary, but to elevate Christ's heavenly priesthood. In this perspective, earthly rituals point toward a transcendent and ultimate reality fulfilled uniquely by Christ's priestly mediation.

The distinctive contribution of chapter eight is its extensive quotation from Jeremiah 31:31–34, marking it as the longest Old Testament citation in the New Testament. This prophetic passage, originally spoken in a context of Israel's exile and hope for renewal, becomes foundational in Hebrews for understanding the "better covenant" mediated by Christ. Jeremiah had envisioned a covenant inscribed not on stone tablets but directly upon human hearts—a profound transformation in humanity's relationship with God.

Hebrews interprets this promise Christologically: the new covenant foretold by Jeremiah finds its definitive realization in Jesus. Unlike the covenant mediated by Moses, which was externally oriented and dependent on continual sacrificial rituals, the new covenant enacted by Christ involves an internal transformation—"I will put my laws in their minds and write them on their hearts" (Heb. 8:10). This internalization implies direct, unmediated intimacy with God: "They will all know me, from the least of them to the greatest" (Heb. 8:11).

The implications of this transformation are significant. First, it radically redefines the nature of divine-human interaction. Knowledge of God is no longer mediated exclusively through priestly rites, law observance, or sacrificial cult, but is accessible directly through the person and work of Christ. Second, it addresses the limitations inherent in the old covenant. Hebrews explicitly notes that the very introduction of a new covenant implies the obsolescence of the old: "By calling this covenant 'new,' he has made the first one obsolete" (Heb. 8:13). This stark language underscores the author's pastoral urgency. The intended audience must recognize that the fulfillment brought about by Christ necessitates moving beyond previous religious forms.

Yet Hebrews is careful not to dismiss or dishonor the old covenant outright. Rather, it insists on continuity even within this transformation. The new covenant fulfills rather than destroys the old; it completes what the previous system anticipated and prepared. Indeed, Jeremiah's prophecy itself emerges from within the heart of the old covenant tradition, thus demonstrating continuity in God's overarching plan. The author's hermeneutic consistently highlights Christ as the culmination of Israel's long covenantal history.

For the first-century community addressed by Hebrews, facing pressures of persecution and potential drift, this vision of a "better covenant" provided theological clarity and pastoral encouragement. It reaffirmed their identity as participants in a profound spiritual transformation, one that surpassed mere adherence to external rituals. Their faithfulness was anchored not in a temple prone to destruction nor in rites requiring constant repetition, but in Christ's permanent, sufficient, and heavenly mediation.

In conclusion, Hebrews chapter 8 presents Christ as the mediator of a new and better covenant, grounded in an enduring spiritual transformation prophesied by Jeremiah. Through Christ, covenantal intimacy with God is internalized, fulfilled, and perfected. The pastoral implications remain potent today, inviting contemporary believers into deeper reflection on how they experience and express their covenant relationship with God through Christ.

Excursus: Hebrews, the New Covenant, and the History of Christian Anti-Judaism

The Epistle to the Hebrews presents Jesus as the mediator of a "new covenant" that surpasses and fulfills the covenant established through Moses (Heb. 8:6–13). Drawing on Jeremiah 31, Hebrews depicts this new covenant as marked by internal transformation, direct knowledge of God, and decisive forgiveness of sins. Within its first-century Jewish-Christian context, this theological claim was a profound affirmation of Christ's significance and a reorientation of covenantal identity around him.

However, over the course of church history, such claims have too often been severed from their Jewish roots and weaponized against the Jewish people.

The doctrine of the new covenant became, in some quarters of the church, a foundation for supersessionism — the idea that the church had permanently replaced Israel as the people of God. This view has historically contributed to a deep legacy of anti-Judaism, which, over time, evolved into or intersected with antisemitism, resulting in real harm to Jewish communities.

Early Christian writings often interpreted the contrast between "old" and "new" in adversarial terms. For instance, some patristic authors described Judaism as a failed or obsolete religion, its covenant rendered void by Christ's coming. This was not necessarily the logic of Hebrews itself, but it became a dominant pattern of interpretation. The language of "better promises," "obsolete covenant," and "shadow vs. reality," as found in Hebrews 8 and 10, was increasingly employed not just to exalt Christ, but to degrade Judaism.

These theological currents contributed to a broader cultural and political environment in which Jews were marginalized, stereotyped, and persecuted. From the theological polemics of figures like John Chrysostom, to medieval restrictions, forced conversions, and expulsions, to the religious justifications used during pogroms, and ultimately to the Holocaust, the legacy of Christian anti-Judaism has had tragic and enduring consequences. While not the sole cause of antisemitism, distorted theological readings of texts like Hebrews have contributed to centuries of hostility and violence.

Given this history, contemporary interpreters of Hebrews face a vital responsibility: to read and teach the text in a way that respects its Jewish context, avoids supersessionist interpretations, and resists the tendency to define Christian identity over and against Judaism.

Several principles can guide this better path:

Contextualizing the Contrast

Hebrews' distinction between old and new covenants arises from within an intra-Jewish context. The author is not critiquing Judaism from the outside but reinterpreting covenantal categories in light of Jesus, whom the community regards as Messiah. The argument presupposes shared reverence for the Scriptures, the temple, and the priesthood. It is a theological reconfiguration, not an ethnic or religious denouncement.

Affirming Continuity as Well as Fulfillment

Hebrews affirms that the new covenant was anticipated within the old. It quotes Jeremiah 31 — written by a Hebrew prophet to the people of Israel — as evidence of God's long-standing intention to renew the covenant from within. This continuity challenges interpretations that pit Christianity and Judaism as diametrically opposed or mutually exclusive.

Rejecting Replacement Theology

A growing number of Christian theologians today advocate for post-supersessionist readings of the New Testament — approaches that affirm the abiding validity of God's covenant with the Jewish people. These interpretations maintain that Gentile believers are incorporated into Israel's story through Christ, not as replacements but as participants in the expansion of God's promises.

Learning from Jewish-Christian Dialogue

In recent decades, renewed dialogue between Jewish and Christian scholars has led to greater mutual understanding. Jewish interpreters have highlighted the shared scriptural heritage of Hebrews and its deep engagement with Jewish thought. Christian readers, in turn, have been challenged to approach texts like Hebrews with greater humility and attentiveness to the dangers of theological triumphalism.

Embracing the Ethic of Hebrews

Ironically, the very themes Hebrews emphasizes—perseverance, humility, access to God through mercy, and priestly compassion—call into question any interpretation that fosters arrogance, superiority, or contempt. The "better covenant" is not a license for pride but an invitation to deeper faithfulness, shaped by the intercession and self-giving love of Christ.

The church's history of anti-Judaism is a sobering backdrop against which to read Hebrews today. While the letter proclaims the surpassing glory of Christ and the promises of the new covenant, it must not be co-opted into narratives that demean or displace the Jewish people. Instead, a careful, faithful reading of

Hebrews can lead to a greater appreciation for its Jewish roots, a more inclusive vision of covenant, and a Christian identity marked not by opposition but by humility, reverence, and shared hope.

Chapter 11
Christ's Once-for-All Sacrifice
(Hebrews 9:1–10:18)

Hebrews chapters 9 and 10 offer one of the richest theological reflections on Christ's sacrifice in the New Testament. Having established Christ's heavenly priesthood and superior covenant, the author now vividly portrays the implications of Christ's sacrifice as a definitive, singular, and unrepeatable event — contrasted sharply with the repeated rituals of the old covenant.

Chapter 9 begins by describing the earthly tabernacle and its rituals (9:1–10). These practices, the author explains, served primarily as symbols, temporary measures that could not achieve lasting purification of conscience. They were external regulations pointing forward to a deeper, more profound purification that could only be achieved through Christ's sacrifice. The tabernacle, with its distinct areas of increasing holiness — the Holy Place and the Most Holy Place — exemplified the separation between humanity and God, necessitating ongoing priestly intercession and continual sacrifices.

Hebrews then dramatically shifts focus from earthly rituals to the heavenly reality. Christ is portrayed as entering not a man-made sanctuary but heaven itself, appearing before God on behalf of humanity (9:11–12). Unlike the Levitical priests, who required the repeated offering of animal blood, Christ offered his own blood, securing an "eternal redemption." This distinction is critical: animal sacrifices were limited, symbolically effective, but ultimately incapable of fully removing guilt or achieving lasting reconciliation. In contrast, Christ's sacrifice achieves true and lasting purification of the human conscience, transforming believers from within.

Central to this argument is the author's reflection on the nature of Christ's death. It is depicted as the ultimate fulfillment of the sacrificial system inaugurated under the Mosaic covenant. By emphasizing the superiority and sufficiency of Christ's offering, Hebrews makes clear that the old system, reliant on repeated sacrifices, is fulfilled and made obsolete by Christ's singular act (9:23–28). Christ's sacrifice, in effect, brings about a new age characterized by direct access to God, marked by internal spiritual renewal and profound assurance of forgiveness.

The imagery intensifies in chapter 10, where the limitations of the old sacrificial system are reiterated: "It is impossible for the blood of bulls and goats to take away sins" (10:4). Repetition of sacrifices highlighted their ineffectiveness and pointed towards something better—a sacrifice that could truly cleanse and sanctify once for all. The author quotes Psalm 40, using the Greek Septuagint (LXX) version, which reads "a body you have prepared for me," rather than the Masoretic Text's "ears you have dug for me." Hebrews utilizes this significant textual difference to underscore the bodily, sacrificial offering of Christ, emphasizing his voluntary and complete self-giving in obedience to God's will. This Christological interpretation establishes a new and lasting covenantal relationship.

Christ's sacrifice, according to Hebrews, accomplishes what the old sacrifices could only symbolize. It achieves genuine sanctification, permanently setting apart believers as holy before God (10:10). The author emphasizes the completed nature of this sacrifice by noting again Christ's seated posture at God's right hand—a powerful symbolic act underscoring completion, finality, and sufficiency (10:12–14).

The pastoral and theological implications of Christ's once-for-all sacrifice are profound. Hebrews 10:18 functions as the practical culmination of the author's intense theological argument, declaring decisively that "where there is forgiveness of these, there is no longer any offering for sin." The theological significance translates directly into practical reality: the sacrificial system involving repeated animal offerings is rendered unnecessary by Christ's completed sacrifice. Thus, Hebrews not only redefines theological understandings but profoundly alters religious practice, confirming that the former methods of atonement are now obsolete due to the comprehensive and final forgiveness achieved through Jesus. Believers are invited into a new covenant characterized by confidence, intimacy, and assurance of permanent reconciliation with God, relying fully on Christ's finished work.

In conclusion, Hebrews 9:1–10:18 provides a definitive reflection on Christ's sacrifice as a transformative, once-for-all event that fulfills and supersedes the old covenantal rituals. Through his singular sacrifice, Christ inaugurates a new covenant characterized by permanent forgiveness, internal sanctification, and direct access to God.

Excursus: Animal Sacrifice in the Ancient World

To fully appreciate the theological significance of Christ's once-for-all sacrifice in Hebrews 9–10, it is important to understand the broader cultural and religious landscape in which animal sacrifice functioned. Far from being a peculiarly Israelite practice, animal sacrifice was a universal phenomenon in the ancient world, spanning cultures, continents, and creeds. For ancient peoples, sacrifice was central to how the divine-human relationship was understood and sustained.

The Logic of Sacrifice

In most ancient societies, sacrifice served as a means of communication with the divine. Animals were offered as gifts to the gods to express thanksgiving, seek favor, atone for wrongdoing, or secure protection. The underlying assumption was that divine beings could be honored and appeased through ritual offerings, especially those that involved blood, fire, and the transformation of physical matter. The act of killing and offering an animal was not merely symbolic; it was thought to establish or restore cosmic order, social harmony, and personal purification.

This logic applied across Mesopotamian, Egyptian, Greek, Roman, and Canaanite religious systems. In Greek religion, for instance, communal sacrifices were often conducted at altars outside temples, involving the burning of select portions and the sharing of the remainder in a ritual meal. Roman religion institutionalized sacrificial rites as integral to civic identity and state stability. In Canaanite practice, sacrifices were linked to fertility, seasonal cycles, and sometimes extreme expressions like child sacrifice — practices from which Israel's Scriptures explicitly distance themselves (e.g., Lev 18:21).

Animal Sacrifice in Israel

While sharing much with its neighbors in terms of sacrificial forms — burnt offerings, peace offerings, sin offerings, and guilt offerings — Israelite sacrificial theology was distinctive in its strict monotheism and covenantal framework. Sacrifices were not offered to secure arbitrary favor but to express covenant fidelity, address impurity, and maintain relational wholeness with Yahweh. Leviticus articulates this theology most fully, where the shedding of blood functions as a means of ritual purification and atonement: "For the life of the flesh is in the blood... it is the blood that makes atonement by the life" (Lev 17:11).

The Day of Atonement (Yom Kippur), referenced explicitly in Hebrews, exemplified this system. Once a year, the high priest entered the Most Holy Place to offer blood on behalf of the entire community, symbolically cleansing both people and sanctuary (Lev 16). This ritual revealed both the gravity of sin and the possibility of reconciliation — but also its impermanence. The repetition of sacrifice, year after year, signaled both the necessity and the inadequacy of the system.

Hebrews and the Critique of Repetition

Against this backdrop, the Epistle to the Hebrews makes a profound theological claim: Christ's offering of himself is qualitatively different from the repeated animal sacrifices of the old covenant. Animal blood could purify the flesh but not the conscience (Heb. 9:13–14). The very repetition of the sacrifices revealed their inability to deal with sin once and for all (10:1–4). Christ's sacrifice, by contrast, is described as "once for all," offered "through the eternal Spirit," effecting complete and permanent redemption (9:12, 14, 26).

The author of Hebrews does not denigrate the old system but regards it as provisional and anticipatory. The animal sacrifices of the Mosaic covenant pointed beyond themselves to a greater reality. They functioned as types — ritual shadows of the substance that would be realized in Christ. In this framework, Jesus' death is not merely one more offering in a long line but the singular, definitive sacrifice that brings true access to God and genuine cleansing of sin.

Animal Sacrifice and Modern Readers

For modern readers, especially those unfamiliar with ancient religious cultures, the prominence of sacrificial language in Hebrews can be challenging or even off-putting. Contemporary sensibilities are far removed from a world in which killing animals was not only religiously meaningful but socially normative. Yet understanding ancient sacrifice as a universal mode of divine-human relationship sheds light on why Hebrews insists so strongly on Christ's sacrificial role.

In the ancient world, the abolition of sacrifice would have been unthinkable. To do away with it would seem to sever the very means by which humanity approached the divine. Hebrews dares to make that claim—not by rejecting sacrifice altogether, but by affirming that in Jesus, sacrifice has reached its climactic fulfillment. No further offering is needed because the one true sacrifice has been made.

Animal sacrifice was foundational to ancient religion, including Israel's. It represented both humanity's deepest longings for divine communion and the persistent problem of sin and estrangement. Hebrews honors that tradition while declaring that Christ's self-offering has fulfilled what animal sacrifice could never achieve. His blood, shed once for all, inaugurates a new and living way into the presence of God—rendering further bloodshed both unnecessary and obsolete. In this way, Hebrews both draws from and transcends the sacrificial world it inhabits, pointing readers to a God who desires not the blood of bulls and goats, but hearts transformed by grace.

Chapter 12
Hold Fast to Faith
Warnings and Examples
(Hebrews 10:19-11:40)

Having thoroughly established the superior priesthood and sacrifice of Christ, the author of Hebrews turns in 10:19 to explicit pastoral exhortation. This section, extending through the famed "Hall of Faith" in chapter 11, marks a shift from theological exposition to urgent encouragement and cautionary warnings. The audience is implored to persevere in faith, grounded in the full assurance provided by Christ's completed work.

Hebrews 10:19-25 initiates this shift by urging believers to confidently enter God's presence, having their hearts purified and consciences cleansed by Christ's sacrifice. The theological implications are practical and immediate: believers must "hold unswervingly to the hope we profess," actively encouraging one another, gathering regularly, and maintaining spiritual vigilance (10:23-25). The author emphasizes communal responsibility, reinforcing that perseverance in faith is not merely individual but deeply corporate.

This pastoral urgency is further underscored by a stark warning against deliberate apostasy in Hebrews

10:26–31. Those who knowingly reject Christ after experiencing the truth face severe consequences. The intensity of this warning serves a rhetorical purpose, highlighting the seriousness of faithfulness and the gravity of abandoning the unique and final sacrifice of Christ. Rather than merely instilling fear, it underscores the irreplaceable significance of Christ's atoning work, pressing believers toward renewed devotion.

Hebrews balances this warning with a reminder of the audience's own history of endurance under persecution and hardship (10:32–39). They had already demonstrated perseverance amidst suffering, publicly exposed to reproach, and willingly sharing in the afflictions of fellow believers. The author affirms their past resilience as evidence of genuine faith, urging continued endurance in anticipation of the promised reward. Thus, past faithfulness becomes both a comfort and a call to continued fidelity.

The celebrated chapter 11 offers a vivid narrative illustration of this perseverance through faith. Often called the "Hall of Faith," it catalogs Old Testament figures whose lives exemplified steadfast trust in God amidst adversity and uncertainty. From Abel and Enoch to Noah, Abraham, Sarah, Moses, and beyond, the list encapsulates a broad spectrum of faithful living: obedience, endurance, sacrifice, and hopeful expectation of promises not fully realized within their lifetimes.

These heroes of faith are depicted not as flawless individuals but as models of persistent reliance on God's promises. Their stories collectively illustrate faith as "confidence in what we hope for and assurance about what we do not see" (11:1). Faith, for Hebrews, is dynamic and active, expressed through tangible acts of obedience, sacrifice, and courage in the face of opposition and suffering.

Hebrews also emphasizes the eschatological dimension of faith—each figure in chapter 11 is characterized by forward-looking expectancy, acknowledging their pilgrim status and anticipating a future city designed and built by God (11:13–16). This orientation provides profound encouragement to the readers, reminding them that faith inherently involves patient waiting and trusting in God's ultimate fulfillment.

Importantly, Hebrews concludes this catalog by highlighting the incomplete nature of these ancient figures' experiences: "These were all commended for their faith, yet none of them received what had been promised, since God had planned something better for us so that only together with us would they be made perfect" (11:39–40). This pivotal statement connects past, present, and future believers, underscoring a unified narrative of redemption culminating in Christ.

The pastoral purpose is clear: the audience is invited to view their own struggles and uncertainties within the broader context of God's faithfulness throughout history. As heirs of this legacy of faith, believers are compelled not to retreat but to press forward confidently, encouraged by the cloud of faithful witnesses who testify to God's unchanging faithfulness and promises.

In summary, Hebrews 10:19–11:40 masterfully integrates exhortation, warning, encouragement, and historical illustration to urge believers toward steadfast endurance in faith. The stories of past heroes reinforce the call to present perseverance, grounding their hope firmly in the faithfulness of God and the completed work of Christ.

Excursus: Faith and Faithfulness in the New Testament — The Richness of Πίστις

The Greek word πίστις (*pistis*) — commonly translated as "faith" — is among the most theologically significant and richly layered terms in the New Testament. At the heart of Christian life and doctrine, *pistis* can convey a range of meanings, from belief or trust to loyalty, fidelity, and steadfastness. The Epistle to the Hebrews, especially in chapter 11, provides a vivid demonstration of this range by portraying faith not merely as intellectual assent but as persistent, courageous, and embodied fidelity to God.

Pistis: A Semantic Field
In classical and Hellenistic Greek usage, *pistis* had a wide semantic range. It could mean:
Trust or confidence in a person or claim (akin to "belief")
Reliability or credibility (as in, "this report is trustworthy")
Loyalty or faithfulness in relationships, especially within patron-client systems or political alliances

In Jewish Greek texts like the Septuagint, pistis also took on covenantal connotations, often aligned with Hebrew terms such as 'emunah, which denotes steadfastness or fidelity. In the Psalms and prophetic writings, God's *pistis* typically refers to God's faithfulness to his promises. Thus, *pistis* could describe both God's unwavering reliability and the human response of trust and loyalty.

Faith or Faithfulness? Interpreting Pistis in the New Testament

When New Testament writers employ *pistis*, they often move fluidly between these meanings. For example:

In Paul's letters, *pistis* can mean trust in God's saving action (Rom. 3:28), but it also connotes a life of covenantal loyalty (Gal. 5:6; 1 Thess. 1:3).

The debate over whether "πίστις Χριστοῦ" (e.g., Gal. 2:16; Rom. 3:22) should be translated as "faith in Christ" (objective genitive) or "faithfulness of Christ" (subjective genitive) exemplifies this complexity. Both renderings are grammatically possible and theologically rich.

In Hebrews 11, *pistis* is presented not as abstract belief but as enduring faithfulness expressed through concrete action. The so-called "Hall of Faith" features individuals who "by faith" obeyed, built, suffered, wandered, and endured. Faith here is not merely believing God exists (cf. Heb. 11:6), but acting in accordance with God's promises despite delay, hardship, or uncertainty. Abel offers. Noah builds.

Abraham leaves. Moses refuses. Rahab welcomes. Each act demonstrates a *pistis* that includes both trust in God and faithful obedience to God's call.

The pastoral message is clear: for Hebrews, *pistis* is not a static quality but a lived orientation toward God — trusting Him for what is unseen and remaining faithful in the midst of testing. It is less about mental certainty and more about relational perseverance.

Chapter 13
Run with Endurance
God's Discipline and Heavenly Citizenship
(Hebrews 12:1-29)

In chapter 12, Hebrews transitions seamlessly from examples of historical faithfulness to direct exhortation about the practical implications of enduring faith. Having drawn inspiration from the "great cloud of witnesses" described previously, the author now calls believers to actively embody this legacy by persevering in their spiritual journey, even amidst hardship and divine discipline.

The chapter begins by vividly employing athletic imagery to emphasize perseverance: "let us throw off everything that hinders and the sin that so easily entangles, and let us run with perseverance the race marked out for us" (12:1). This metaphor effectively conveys the rigorous effort, focused commitment, and disciplined determination required of believers. Crucially, the author directs their attention to Jesus as the exemplar of endurance, who "for the joy set before him endured the cross, scorning its shame, and sat down at the right hand of the throne of God" (12:2). Thus, Christ is not only the object of faith but also its supreme model, demonstrating endurance in suffering for the sake of future glory.

Hebrews further explores the theme of suffering by reframing it through the lens of divine discipline (12:5–11). Quoting Proverbs 3:11–12, the author portrays hardships as evidence of God's paternal care rather than divine neglect. Discipline, though painful, is portrayed positively, as a sign of genuine relationship with God who seeks spiritual maturity and holiness for His children. This perspective transforms experiences of adversity from mere obstacles into meaningful opportunities for growth, urging believers to respond with patience, resilience, and trust.

The exhortation moves from personal endurance to corporate responsibility in 12:12–17. Believers are urged to support each other in their collective race, ensuring that no one falls short of God's grace through bitterness, immorality, or spiritual negligence. The example of Esau serves as a sobering warning against the dangers of immediate gratification and careless disregard for one's spiritual inheritance. This reminder reinforces the seriousness with which believers must treat their communal and individual spiritual responsibilities.

In the climactic section of chapter 12 (verses 18–29), Hebrews contrasts the fear and inaccessibility of Sinai with the joyful and welcoming reality of Mount Zion. Under the new covenant, believers do not approach God in trembling fear associated with the Mosaic law but with joyous confidence, celebrating their status as citizens of a heavenly Jerusalem. This portrayal of Zion vividly underscores the security, permanence, and spiritual privilege inherent in the believers' new relationship with God through Christ.

Nevertheless, the author concludes with a solemn reminder that this heavenly privilege does not imply casual familiarity or diminished reverence. God remains "a consuming fire" (12:29), and the kingdom believers inherit is ultimately "unshakable" precisely because of God's holy character and sovereign authority. Thus, the appropriate response is a life characterized by reverent worship, awe, and profound gratitude, balancing confident joy with humble reverence.

In sum, Hebrews 12 powerfully synthesizes personal exhortation, communal responsibility, and eschatological promise. By interpreting adversity as purposeful divine discipline and emphasizing believers' privileged heavenly citizenship, it urges an active, disciplined perseverance rooted firmly in both Christ's example and the enduring promises of God.

Excursus: The Meaning of Παιδεία in the Ancient World and in Hebrews

In classical Greek thought, paideia referred to the educational, moral, and civic formation of a person, especially a young male citizen. It involved not only instruction in language, literature, and philosophy, but also the cultivation of virtue, discipline, and endurance. The aim of paideia was to shape a person's character and habits so they could fulfill their social and moral responsibilities. The process was rigorous, involving effort, training, correction, and sometimes hardship. But its purpose was always constructive: to produce maturity, wisdom, and excellence (aretē).

This concept remained influential in Hellenistic Judaism. The book of Proverbs, widely read in the Jewish diaspora, commended the discipline of the Lord as a sign of love and a path to wisdom (e.g., Prov. 3:11–12). The Septuagint—the Greek translation of the Hebrew Bible—uses παιδεία repeatedly to render Hebrew terms related to correction, instruction, and upbringing. Paideia, then, was already familiar to many first-century Jewish readers as both a philosophical ideal and a covenantal pattern of God's engagement with His people.

Hebrews 12:5–11 draws directly on Proverbs 3:11–12, quoting the passage to anchor its call to endurance in Scripture:

"My child, do not regard lightly the discipline (παιδεία) of the Lord... for the Lord disciplines those whom he loves." (Heb. 12:5–6)

The author then builds a theological argument grounded in familial imagery: just as earthly fathers discipline their children out of love and responsibility, so too does God discipline those He calls "sons." To experience divine παιδεία, then, is not to be rejected but to be recognized as a legitimate child of God (Heb. 12:7–8).

The tone here is pastoral, not punitive. Hebrews is not suggesting that all suffering is divinely ordained correction, but rather that the experience of hardship can be understood as part of God's formative process. It is a call to interpret suffering not as abandonment but as opportunity: an invitation to spiritual growth, moral refinement, and deeper relational trust in God.

The chapter affirms that this process is difficult: "For the moment all discipline seems painful rather than pleasant" (12:11). Yet it insists that the outcome—"the peaceful fruit of righteousness"—justifies the labor. Like an athlete undergoing training or a student under rigorous instruction, the believer endures not for the pain itself, but for the excellence it produces.

Chapter 14
Living Outside the Camp
Ethics, Community, and Worship
(Hebrews 13:1–25)

Hebrews chapter 13 continues the ethical exhortation of the epistle, emphasizing how theological truths translate into everyday community life. After extensively outlining the profound spiritual and theological realities of Christ's priesthood, sacrifice, and covenant, the author concludes with clear, practical instructions regarding ethical living, community responsibilities, and worship practices. This final chapter underscores the continuity between belief and behavior, urging believers to embody their heavenly citizenship through concrete actions.

The chapter begins with a succinct but powerful exhortation: "Keep on loving one another as brothers and sisters" (13:1). Love, consistently presented as central in New Testament ethics, is here given priority as the defining characteristic of Christian community. The call extends specifically to hospitality toward strangers, recalling examples from Scripture of individuals who unknowingly entertained angels (13:2). Such hospitality signifies openness, generosity, and the breaking down of social barriers, reflecting Christ's inclusive love.

Further ethical instructions follow, highlighting compassionate solidarity with those suffering persecution or imprisonment (13:3), maintaining purity in marital relationships (13:4), and cultivating contentment free from greed (13:5). Each instruction grounds ethical behavior firmly in theological reasoning—God's faithfulness and presence undergird the believer's ethical choices, empowering them to reject materialism and immorality confidently.

Hebrews notably emphasizes the importance of honoring and submitting to community leaders who faithfully proclaim God's word (13:7, 17). Believers are encouraged to observe and emulate their leaders' lives of faithfulness and consistency. At the same time, leaders are reminded of their responsibility to shepherd carefully, knowing they will give an account before God. This mutual accountability fosters a community marked by trust, integrity, and spiritual maturity.

The centrality of Christ's unchanging nature is succinctly reaffirmed: "Jesus Christ is the same yesterday and today and forever" (13:8). This statement anchors the ethical exhortations in Christ's consistent character and dependable faithfulness. Because Christ does not change, believers are encouraged to remain steadfast in their faith and practice, resisting theological novelties or external religious pressures that diverge from the core teachings of the gospel (13:9).

Hebrews 13:10–16 continues to blend theological reflection with practical worship. The author contrasts worship centered in Christ's sacrificial offering with the practices of the earlier covenant. Believers are called to bear Christ's reproach, metaphorically "going outside the camp," indicating a willingness to embrace marginalization for their identification with Christ. True worship, according to Hebrews, consists not merely in ritual acts but in acts of kindness, generosity, and ethical living, described as sacrifices pleasing to God (13:15–16).

The chapter concludes with personal remarks, prayer requests, and benedictions (13:18–25), reinforcing the relational and communal dimensions of faithfulness. These final greetings emphasize the bonds of affection, care, and interdependence within the community of faith, urging believers to pray for one another and for their spiritual leaders.

Hebrews ends with a beautiful and theologically rich benediction, invoking the God of peace who raised Jesus from the dead to equip believers for every good work (13:20–21). This prayer encapsulates the central themes of the epistle: the sufficiency of Christ's sacrifice, the transformative power of the new covenant, and the call to ethical living empowered by God's grace.

In sum, Hebrews chapter 13 integrates ethical exhortation, practical community responsibilities, and authentic worship, illustrating how profound theological insights must inevitably manifest in daily living. By linking ethics directly to Christ's unchanging character and finished work, the author compellingly demonstrates that genuine faith is consistently revealed through loving actions, community fidelity, and worshipful obedience.

Excursus: Persecution in Early Christianity — A Context for Hebrews' Ethical Vision

Throughout the Epistle to the Hebrews, and especially in its exhortative climax in chapter 13, the tone is urgent, pastoral, and ethical. The community is called to mutual love, hospitality, compassion for the imprisoned, sexual purity, contentment, and respect for leaders. These instructions are not merely abstract virtues — they are responses to the lived experience of a community under pressure. Hebrews offers these commands in the shadow of persecution, marginalization, and suffering.

Understanding the nature of persecution in early Christianity — its forms, causes, and psychological impact — can help modern readers grasp both the sharpness and tenderness of Hebrews' exhortations. Unlike later centuries in which Christians faced official, empire-wide persecution under rulers like Decius or Diocletian, the opposition described in Hebrews reflects a local, social, and unofficial form of pressure. Hebrews 10:32–34 recalls earlier experiences of public disgrace, material loss, and solidarity with those in prison:

> You endured a hard struggle with sufferings, sometimes being publicly exposed to abuse and persecution… For you had compassion for those who were in prison, and you cheerfully accepted the plundering of your possessions.

This passage suggests that the community had already suffered for their faith, though likely not yet to the point of martyrdom. Hebrews 12:4 confirms this: "In your struggle against sin you have not yet resisted to the point of shedding your blood."

The nature of this suffering likely included social alienation, loss of legal or economic standing, and local hostility—rather than formal legal prosecution. Evidence from outside the New Testament supports this pattern. A famous example appears in the correspondence between Pliny the Younger, Roman governor of Bithynia-Pontus (in modern-day Turkey), and the Emperor Trajan, around 112 CE.

In Pliny's Letter to Trajan (Ep. 10.96–97), Pliny describes how he has been encountering Christians in his province and is unsure how to proceed. He does not seek them out proactively but investigates when accusations are made. Christians are interrogated and, if they persist in their confession, may be punished— though those who recant and worship the Roman gods are spared. Pliny notes that he required suspected Christians to offer incense and wine to the image of the emperor and to curse Christ—tests of loyalty that Christians typically refused.

Crucially, Pliny reports that the "contagion" of Christianity had spread not only in the cities but even in rural areas, and that former pagans were abandoning temples and traditional sacrifices. Trajan, in response, instructs Pliny not to hunt Christians actively, but to punish them if formally accused and proven guilty.

This correspondence illustrates several key features of the early persecution Christians faced:

It was regional and case-specific, dependent on the attitude of local governors.

The primary offense was not holding unorthodox beliefs per se, but failing to honor Roman religious norms—especially emperor worship.

Accusations could arise from social resentment, religious suspicion, or political tension.

Though Pliny's letter postdates Hebrews by several decades, it reflects the kind of unpredictable, civic hostility and religious marginalization that Hebrews' audience may have been experiencing. Their suffering was not yet martyrdom, but it was real: economic pressure, loss of status, threats of imprisonment, and the ongoing temptation to return to more socially acceptable forms of religion.

Chapter 15
Canonical Status and Historical Reception

The Epistle to the Hebrews occupies a unique position within the development of the New Testament canon. Its anonymity, complex theology, and stylistic distinctiveness set it apart from other apostolic writings. Yet despite — or perhaps because of — these distinctive qualities, Hebrews exerted deep influence on early Christian theology, liturgy, and ecclesial identity. This chapter traces the evolving reception of Hebrews, examining how it came to be included in the canon and the theological weight it has carried across generations.

It is important to recognize that the concept of a fixed New Testament canon did not fully emerge until the fourth century. Prior to this period, early Christian communities were engaged in fluid and localized processes of textual usage and theological discernment. Thus, the reception of Hebrews before the fourth century should not be described in terms of simple acceptance or rejection. Rather, Hebrews' early use — and, at times, lack of use — reflects broader patterns of scriptural formation, liturgical incorporation, and theological resonance.

Hebrews is notably absent from some early lists of authoritative writings and is underrepresented in citations from some second-century writers. The

Muratorian Fragment, whose precise date and provenance remain debated, does not include Hebrews. This omission may reflect hesitations related to authorship, geographic usage, or the evolving nature of manuscript collections. The uncertainties surrounding the fragment's context also caution against drawing definitive conclusions about Hebrews' status across all early Christian communities. Nevertheless, such omissions do not necessarily indicate rejection.

One key difference in Hebrews' early reception lies between Greek and Latin manuscript traditions. Hebrews was included consistently in Greek collections of Paul's letters but was initially excluded from Latin ones. This difference likely had more to do with scribal practices and manuscript transmission than with formal theological decisions. The diversity of reception across manuscript traditions illustrates that early Christian attitudes toward Hebrews were shaped as much by practical and regional factors as by doctrinal judgments.

In the Greek-speaking communities, Hebrews gained traction at least by the third century. Clement of Alexandria accepted it as Pauline, suggesting that Paul originally wrote the letter in Hebrew and that Luke translated it into Greek. Origen, while acknowledging the uncertainty of authorship — "Who wrote the epistle, in truth God knows" — nevertheless valued its theological depth and spiritual insight. Its integration into Greek codices of Paul's letters helped reinforce its use and authority.

In contrast, the Latin-speaking communities appear to have been slower to embrace Hebrews as

Pauline. The early Latin tradition did not include Hebrews in Pauline collections, and questions about its authorship lingered. Yet, over time, influential figures such as Jerome and Augustine came to affirm its inclusion, even while acknowledging debates about its authorship and authority. The councils of Hippo (393) and Carthage (397) included Hebrews in their lists of New Testament writings.

Upon achieving broad acceptance, Hebrews began to exert wide influence on theology, liturgy, and ecclesial structure. Its depiction of Christ as high priest shaped early Christian understandings of Jesus' heavenly ministry and atonement. The letter's emphasis on perseverance and covenant fidelity resonated deeply within monastic and pastoral traditions. In Eastern liturgies, Hebrews was sometimes read during Holy Week, its themes of sacrifice and priesthood aligning with the Passion narrative.

Patristic theologians drew heavily on Hebrews. Athanasius cited it in defense of Nicene Christology. John Chrysostom delivered homilies on Hebrews that were influential in the later interpretative tradition. Thomas Aquinas later incorporated Hebrews into systematic theology, producing an influential commentary.

In sum, the canonical status and reception of Hebrews illustrate a dynamic and multilayered process. Rather than a story of simple inclusion or exclusion, Hebrews' journey into the canon reflects the complex interplay of manuscript tradition, theological resonance, and ecclesial usage. What began as an anonymous homily eventually came to be recognized as sacred Scripture—not because of its provenance alone, but because of its power to speak Christ into the life of the church.

Chapter 16
Modern Approaches to Hebrews

The Epistle to the Hebrews has long challenged interpreters with its anonymous authorship, distinctive style, and intricate theology. In recent decades, the letter has attracted renewed scholarly interest across a broad spectrum of methodological approaches. This chapter explores several of the most influential contemporary frameworks for studying Hebrews, including historical-critical analysis, rhetorical and narrative criticism, and various ideological readings such as feminist, postcolonial, and liberationist approaches. Each of these perspectives highlights different dimensions of the text and contributes to a richer understanding of its theological, literary, and cultural significance.

Historical-critical approaches continue to shape the academic study of Hebrews, particularly in efforts to reconstruct the letter's historical context and trace its use of scriptural sources. Scholars working within this tradition have analyzed Hebrews' engagement with the Septuagint (LXX), its conceptual background in Second Temple Judaism, and its theological dialogue with early Christian communities. The focus here is often on situating Hebrews within the diverse landscape of early Christianity and understanding how its argument emerges from and responds to contemporary religious developments. These studies highlight Hebrews' deep intertextuality and sophisticated reinterpretation of Israel's scriptures, especially in its presentation of Christ as both high priest and mediator.

Rhetorical criticism has proven especially fruitful for interpreting Hebrews. Building on the recognition that Hebrews reads more like a sermon than a traditional letter, scholars have examined its structure, rhetorical strategies, and persuasive techniques. Attention has been given to its use of comparisons (synkrisis), its alternation between exhortation and exposition, and its appeals to the emotions and experiences of the audience. These studies underscore the epistle's pastoral intent, showing how theological claims are embedded in a carefully crafted appeal to the community's endurance, commitment, and hope.

Closely related are narrative-critical approaches, which focus on how Hebrews constructs a coherent story world and invites readers to inhabit it. These interpretations view the epistle not simply as a collection of arguments but as a theological narrative that recasts the history of Israel, redefines covenant and priesthood, and situates the audience within an eschatological drama. Such approaches highlight the letter's temporal complexity — its emphasis on what has been fulfilled, what is presently accessible through faith, and what is still to come.

In recent decades, ideological and contextual readings have opened new avenues for engaging Hebrews. Feminist scholars have examined the letter's use of patriarchal imagery, its male-dominated exemplars of faith, and the absence of female voices. While some have critiqued Hebrews for reinforcing hierarchical and exclusionary patterns, others have explored the subversive potential of its theology, particularly in its vision of solidarity, marginalization, and transformation.

Postcolonial and liberationist interpreters have similarly found both challenge and promise in Hebrews. The epistle's emphasis on "going outside the camp" (13:13) and enduring reproach has been read as a call to identification with the oppressed and marginalized. At the same time, the text's frequent use of hierarchical language have raised questions about how Hebrews might be read both critically and constructively in contexts of power and resistance. These readings invite continued reflection on the socio-political implications of theological discourse.

Reception history has become another vibrant area of study, tracing how Hebrews has been interpreted and deployed across time and tradition. From patristic exegesis to medieval monastic use, from Reformation debates to modern liturgical contexts, scholars have explored how different communities have appropriated Hebrews' themes of priesthood, sacrifice, and perseverance. Reception history reveals the diversity of Hebrews' afterlives and the ways its meaning has been shaped by shifting historical and theological concerns.

Finally, theological interpretations of Hebrews continue to engage the epistle as a living voice within Christian theology. Contemporary theologians have drawn on Hebrews to reflect on issues such as Christology, atonement, ecclesiology, and eschatology. The letter's depiction of Jesus as the pioneer and perfecter of faith, its vision of heavenly worship, and its sustained call to perseverance have resonated across traditions as resources for both doctrinal reflection and spiritual formation.

In sum, modern approaches to Hebrews reflect a wide and growing field of inquiry. Whether through critical reconstruction, literary analysis, ideological engagement, or theological appropriation, scholars continue to find in Hebrews a rich and provocative witness to early Christian faith and imagination. These diverse readings ensure that Hebrews remains not only a subject of historical interest but a text that continues to speak into new contexts and questions.

Chapter 17
Study Questions and Exercises

This chapter provides a set of study tools designed to reinforce learning, provoke critical thinking, and support individual or group engagement with the Epistle to the Hebrews. These exercises are particularly suited for classroom settings, church study groups, or independent readers seeking a structured approach.

Discussion Questions

How does Hebrews 1 contrast the Son with the angels, and why is this significant?

What themes of solidarity and priesthood are introduced in chapters 2–4?

How does Hebrews reframe the figure of Melchizedek in chapters 5–7?

In what ways does Hebrews 8 redefine covenant in light of Christ?

What theological and pastoral implications arise from the "once-for-all" sacrifice in chapters 9–10?

How do the examples in Hebrews 11 serve the broader exhortation to endure?

What does Hebrews 12 suggest about divine discipline and communal perseverance?

How does the final chapter (13) summarize and apply the ethical and communal vision of the letter?

Thematic Essay Prompts

Analyze the Christological claims of Hebrews and how they relate to the Old Testament.

Compare Hebrews' use of Scripture with other New Testament writings.

Explore the rhetorical structure and flow of argument in Hebrews.

Discuss the tension between warning and encouragement in the letter's pastoral strategy.

Research Paper Ideas

The role of the heavenly sanctuary motif in Hebrews.

An exploration of faith in Hebrews 11 in light of ancient Jewish literature.

Hebrews' reception in patristic theology and liturgy.

A comparative study of Hebrews and Pauline epistles on the theme of covenant.

Exegetical Exercises

Conduct a close reading of Hebrews 4:14–16. What is the significance of approaching the throne of grace?

Analyze Hebrews 10:19–25. How does the passage function as a bridge in the letter?

Examine the quotation of Jeremiah 31 in Hebrews 8. How is it reinterpreted Christologically?

These exercises aim to encourage deeper engagement with the text and equip readers to interpret Hebrews both critically and devotionally.

Select Bibliography

Attridge, Harold W. *The Epistle to the Hebrews*.
Hermeneia. Philadelphia: Fortress Press, 1989.

Bauckham, Richard, Daniel R. Driver, Trevor A. Hart,
& Nathan MacDonald, eds. *The Epistle to the
Hebrews and Christian Theology*. Grand Rapids:
Eerdmans, 2009.

Cockerill, Gareth Lee. *The Epistle to the Hebrews*. New
International Commentary on the New
Testament. Grand Rapids: Eerdmans, 2012.

Cosby, Michael R. *Apostle to the Conquered: Reimagining
Paul's Mission*. Grand Rapids: Eerdmans, 2005.

DeSilva, David A. *Perseverance in Gratitude: A Socio-
Rhetorical Commentary on the Epistle to the
Hebrews*. Grand Rapids: Eerdmans, 2000.

Dunnill, John. *Covenant and Sacrifice in the Letter to the
Hebrews*. Society for New Testament Studies
Monograph Series 75. Cambridge: Cambridge
University Press, 1992.

Guthrie, George H. *The Structure of Hebrews: A Text-
Linguistic Analysis*. Novum Testamentum
Supplements 73. Leiden: Brill, 1994.

Hagner, Donald A. *Encountering the Book of Hebrews: An
Expository Survey*. Grand Rapids: Baker
Academic, 2002.

Isaacs, Marie E. *Sacred Space: An Approach to the Theology of the Epistle to the Hebrews*. Journal for the Study of the New Testament Supplement Series 73. Sheffield: Sheffield Academic Press, 1992.

Johnson, Luke Timothy. *Hebrews: A Commentary*. New Testament Library. Louisville: Westminster John Knox Press, 2006.

Koester, Craig R. *Hebrews: A New Translation with Introduction and Commentary*. Anchor Yale Bible 36. New Haven: Yale University Press, 2001.

Lane, William L. *Hebrews 1–8* and *Hebrews 9–13*. Word Biblical Commentary 47A–B. Dallas: Word Books, 1991.

Mason, Eric F., and Kevin B. McCruden, eds. *Reading the Epistle to the Hebrews: A Resource for Students*. Atlanta: Society of Biblical Literature, 2011.

Moffitt, David M. *Atonement and the Logic of Resurrection in the Epistle to the Hebrews*. Supplements to the Journal for the Study of Judaism 141. Leiden: Brill, 2011.

Rhee, Victor (Sung-Yul). *Faith in Hebrews: Analysis within the Context of Christology, Eschatology, and Ethics*. Studies in Biblical Literature 65. New York: Peter Lang, 2001.

Rothschild, Clare K. *Hebrews as Pseudepigraphon: The History and Significance of the Pauline Attribution*. Wissenschaftliche Untersuchungen zum Neuen Testament 235. Tübingen: Mohr Siebeck, 2009.

Schreiner, Thomas R. *Commentary on Hebrews*. Biblical Theology for Christian Proclamation. Nashville: B&H Academic, 2015.

Thompson, James W. *Hebrews*. Paideia Commentaries on the New Testament. Grand Rapids: Baker Academic, 2008.

Young, David. *The Concept of Canon in the Reception of the Epistle to the Hebrews*. The Library of New Testament Studies. London: T&T Clark, 2022.

Appendix A

Timeline of Hebrews' Reception

ca. 60–90: Probable date of Hebrews' composition.

2nd century: Fragmentary use by church fathers; not listed in the Muratorian Fragment.

3rd–4th centuries: Widespread acceptance in Greek collections of Pauline letters.

Late 4th century: Inclusion in Latin canon lists (e.g., Councils of Hippo and Carthage).

Patristic period onward: Regular use in theological reflection, liturgy, and ecclesial instruction.

Appendix B

Glossary of Key Terms

Apostasy: The act of abandoning the faith; a repeated concern in Hebrews.

Christology: The theological study of the person and work of Christ; Hebrews makes significant contributions to early Christian Christology.

Covenant: A divinely instituted relationship between God and humanity; in Hebrews, the old covenant is contrasted with the new covenant inaugurated through Christ.

Day of Atonement: The annual ritual under the old covenant involving sacrifice and priestly mediation; a backdrop for understanding Christ's once-for-all offering.

Exhortation: Urgent pastoral appeal; Hebrews is described as a "word of exhortation."

Faith: Defined in Hebrews 11 as assurance and conviction; a key theme throughout the epistle.

High Priest: A central title for Christ in Hebrews; indicates his role as mediator before God on behalf of humanity.

Melchizedek: A mysterious priest-king in Genesis 14 and Psalm 110, interpreted typologically in Hebrews as a pattern for Christ's priesthood.

Sanctuary: The holy place of worship; Hebrews contrasts the earthly sanctuary with the heavenly one entered by Christ.

Septuagint (LXX): The Greek translation of the Hebrew Bible used extensively in Hebrews' citations and interpretations.

Typology: A method of interpretation in which Old Testament figures or events foreshadow realities fulfilled in Christ.

Warning Passages: Texts in Hebrews (e.g., 6:4–6; 10:26–31) that caution against apostasy and stress the seriousness of perseverance.

Appendix C

Selected OT Texts Quoted in Hebrews

This appendix provides a selection of significant Old Testament passages cited in Hebrews, with commentary on their original context and how the author of Hebrews reinterprets them Christologically.

Genesis 2:2

ORIGINAL CONTEXT: Describes God's rest on the seventh day after creation.

USE IN HEBREWS: Cited in Hebrews 4:4 to support the concept of a sabbath rest for the people of God. Hebrews reinterprets this rest typologically as a spiritual rest available to believers through faith and obedience in Christ.

Genesis 14:18–20

ORIGINAL CONTEXT: Tells of Melchizedek, king of Salem and priest of God Most High, who blesses Abram.

USE IN HEBREWS: Forms the basis of Hebrews 7, where Melchizedek is presented as a type of Christ — eternal, without genealogy, and superior to the Levitical priests. Hebrews uses this narrative to ground the idea of Jesus' priesthood being "according to the order of Melchizedek."

Exodus 19:12–13
ORIGINAL CONTEXT: God warns Israel to keep their distance from Mount Sinai at the giving of the law.
USE IN HEBREWS: Alluded to in Hebrews 12:18–21 to contrast the fearsome, inaccessible Sinai with the welcoming vision of Mount Zion. This contrast emphasizes the superiority of the new covenant and the believer's access to God.

Exodus 24:8
ORIGINAL CONTEXT: Moses sprinkles the blood of the covenant on the people to ratify God's covenant at Sinai.
USE IN HEBREWS: Quoted in Hebrews 9:20 as a parallel to Christ's sacrificial blood. The author contrasts the limited and external effects of Mosaic rituals with the internal and eternal cleansing achieved by Christ.

Deuteronomy 32:35–36
ORIGINAL CONTEXT: God declares God's role as the righteous judge of God's people.
USE IN HEBREWS: Cited in Hebrews 10:30 as part of a stern warning about judgment for those who spurn the grace offered in Christ. The passage reinforces divine justice and retribution against apostasy.

Psalm 8:4–6

ORIGINAL CONTEXT: Reflects on human beings' surprising dignity and status within God's creation.
USE IN HEBREWS: Quoted in Hebrews 2:6–8 to affirm Jesus' full identification with humanity and his ultimate exaltation over all things. The psalm becomes a lens to see Christ as the true human who fulfills God's intention for humanity.

Psalm 22:22

ORIGINAL CONTEXT: A cry for deliverance turns into a declaration of praise and proclamation among the faithful.
USE IN HEBREWS: Cited in Hebrews 2:12 as part of the argument that Jesus shares in the sufferings and experiences of his brothers and sisters. The quotation highlights Jesus' role as one who leads a redeemed community in worship.

Psalm 40:6–8

ORIGINAL CONTEXT: Expresses the psalmist's understanding that obedience is more pleasing to God than sacrifice.
USE IN HEBREWS: Quoted in Hebrews 10:5–7, using the LXX version that says "a body you have prepared for me." This crucial difference allows Hebrews to present Christ as the one who offers perfect obedience through his incarnate body, fulfilling what God truly desires.

Psalm 95:7–11

ORIGINAL CONTEXT: Warns the wilderness generation not to harden their hearts and miss God's rest.

USE IN HEBREWS: Cited in Hebrews 3:7–11 and developed in chapter 4 as a warning to the contemporary audience. The "rest" is reinterpreted as a still-available promise, urging readers to respond with faith.

Psalm 102:25–27

ORIGINAL CONTEXT: A declaration of God's eternal nature amid human frailty.

USE IN HEBREWS: Quoted in Hebrews 1:10–12 and applied to the Son, asserting Christ's divine immutability and superiority over creation.

Psalm 110:1, 4

ORIGINAL CONTEXT: Celebrates the enthronement of a royal priestly figure.

USE IN HEBREWS: Repeatedly cited to establish Christ's royal authority (1:13) and eternal priesthood (5:6; 7:17, 21). Psalm 110 serves as a cornerstone of Hebrews' Christology and argument for Jesus' unique status.

Isaiah 8:17–18

ORIGINAL CONTEXT: Isaiah expresses his trust in God and identifies himself and his children as signs to Israel.

USE IN HEBREWS: Quoted in Hebrews 2:13 to affirm Jesus' solidarity with humanity. Just as Isaiah stands among his people, so does Jesus identify fully with those he redeems.

Jeremiah 31:31–34

ORIGINAL CONTEXT: Announces a future new covenant written on the heart, marked by forgiveness and internal transformation.

USE IN HEBREWS: Quoted in full in Hebrews 8:8–12 and referenced again in 10:16–17. Hebrews presents Jesus as the mediator of this promised new covenant, which replaces the old and brings the forgiveness and intimacy with God that the old system could not secure.

Habakkuk 2:3–4

ORIGINAL CONTEXT: A call to wait patiently for God's justice, emphasizing that the righteous will live by faith.

USE IN HEBREWS: Quoted in Hebrews 10:37–38 as part of the call to perseverance. It supports the idea that continued faithfulness, even in delay or suffering, is the mark of righteousness.

www.ingramcontent.com/pod-product-compliance
Lightning Source LLC
La Vergne TN
LVHW021359080426
835508LV00020B/2349